BARNYARD LEGENDS

JUDITH ZEHNER
KIMBERLEY MOSHER

Sheep's in the meadow,
Cow's in the corn,
Pig's in the clover,
All's right with the morn!

Animas
Quilts
Publishing

600 Main Ave.
Durango, CO 81301
(970) 247-2582

BARNYARD LEGENDS

Animas Quilts Publishing
600 Main Ave.
Durango, CO 81301
(970) 247-2582

ISBN: 1-885156-21-9

Printed on Recycled Paper

Cover Quilt:
    Fred and Sonny
        Judith Zehner
        Kimberley Mosher

Back Cover:
    Art and the Chickens
        Judith Zehner
        Kimberley Mosher

CREDITS:

Editor   Kim Gjere
Graphics   Jackie Robinson
Photography Christopher Marona

THE AUTHORS:

Judy Zehner and Kim Mosher, a Mother-Daughter team, are from rural Routt County and Steamboat Springs, Colorado. Kim was raised on the farm that has been in her Dad's family for three generations. Kim and her brothers, David and Darren, are the fourth generation, and their children the fifth! The family raised all of these animals at one time or another, and are very familiar with the fun, frustrations, and characteristics of animals on the farm. Judy and Kim have written one other book, *Quilted Legends of the West*. They are both busy developing new designs, quilting, teaching, and lecturing.

DEDICATION:

Ayliffe Elizabeth Jones Zehner
May 21, 1906 -
January 21, 1996

We dedicate this book to Ayliffe, Judy's mother-in-law for thirty-six years, and Kim's grandmother. Ayliffe treasured her childhood on the farm in Colorado where her family still lives. Pets and animals were dear to her and lived forever in her memories. She was very proud of our quilting endeavors and was enjoying finding vintage photographs for us to use in this book.

ACKNOWLEDGEMENTS:

We thank our families for their understanding, support, and love; our dear friends; and the Delectable Mountains Quilters Guild, for their assistance.

INTRODUCTION

The American farmer and rancher make it possible today to choose among an abundance never before seen in this world. The knowledge of how to grow crops and tend herds and flocks is more important than ever in a world that faces the prospect of too little for so many on a crowded globe.

Yet, amid the vital importance of it all, are the cherished opportunities to see the miracle of birth and the joyful play of foal, calf, lamb, and kid. The touch and smell of the animals as they are fed, milked, ridden, or worked lingers in our agrarian memory.

Where there is life, there is death; and the death of an animal by design, accident or necessity is a solemn experience. The lessons learned by the care of animals are lessons of life, to be remembered always.

We hope to awaken in each of you the memory of that special day on a farm when you——
  chased the chickens,
    rode the pony,
      fed the lamb,
        held the piglet,
          petted the dog,
            found the kittens,
              saw the sow,
                heard the rooster,
                  watched the birds,
                    sheared the sheep,
                      or gathered the eggs.

Our quilt designs of farm animals emerge from our life's experience on the farm. We had fun drawing these charming designs and we want you to have fun making them. Make them tell your story of that cherished childhood experience, for the special baby, or for that person in your life for whom the animal has particular significance.

We have planned these patterns so that you can create your own farm scenes, putting animals together as you wish and designing your own borders. The birds, the chickens, the lambs, the kids, and the piglets are planned to be used as borders, as well as on backgrounds. Use your imagination and combine them as you choose! After you have made one of our planned designs, we encourage you and challenge you to draft your own arrangement of the animals. The fun is just beginning!

SEWING SUPPLIES

Common quilting tools are all you need to make these quilts. They are as follows:

Sewing machine
Rotary cutter and mat
6" x 24" ruler
6" x 12" ruler
6" x 6" ruler
Small, glass-head pins
Sharp #2 pencil
Assorted marking pencils
Seam ripper
Scissors
1" Safety Pins
2" Binder Clips
Iron and ironing board or
    pressing pad
Design board if desired -
    As the units are assembled,
    you can pin them up and
    watch your farm animal
    come to life.

Read and understand the General Directions before beginning your project. The techniques explained in this section will be referred to often.

FABRIC SELECTION

Isn't it fun to select fabrics with a "country feel?" Country means different things to different people, creating the glorious diversity of choices. The most important consideration is pattern, color, and contrast, so that the animals are identifiable. Directional patterns are more difficult to use, as they must be cut to keep the particular pattern constant, which takes time. It can be done, but we don't recommend using them until you are experienced with our patterns and techniques.

We recommend good quality, 100% cotton fabric, because the performance is predictable. Furry, fuzzy and otherwise "animal" fabrics are thick or slick, so we avoid them.

Some of our creatures use only small amounts of fabrics, so you can use many different patterns from your fabric collection. The more you use, the more "farm-frugal" look you will get.

Yardage is based on 42" wide fabric. Yardage given is actual needed, plus 10% for shrinkage and small cutting errors. In some cases only a scrap or one strip is required, and this is stated. Border yardage is based on cross grain strips; lengthwise strips usually require more fabric. Backing yardage includes a 2" margin around the quilt and 3% for shrinkage. Binding yardage is based on 2-1/2" cross grain strips.

ROTARY CUTTING

All fabric strips and pieces are cut with a rotary cutter and acrylic ruler. Use a rotary mat that has a 1" grid of squares, to help align the fabric.

Lay out the fabric as it comes from the bolt. Bring the folded edge up even with the selvage edges. Smooth any wrinkles out to both ends. Align the folded edge on a grid line of the mat. Cut the edge of the fabric perpendicular to the folded edge. Keep the folded edge of fabric even with the grid line on the mat to assure that the strips are cut squarely. Check the cut edge periodically to make sure it is still perpendicular to the folded edge, cutting again if necessary.

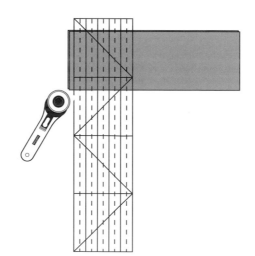

Hold the rotary cutter perpendicular to the mat. Slanting either inward or outward will alter the width of the strip. Cut the strips as listed in the cutting chart.

SEAM ALLOWANCE

It is important to sew a true 1/4" seam allowance. Either adjust the needle on the sewing machine to sew 1/4", use a 1/4" foot, or use tape on the throat plate to mark 1/4". Test your 1/4" before beginning your project.

PINNING

With patience and practice you will be able to match seams perfectly. Use fine, glass-head pins. Large quilting pins distort the fabric. Seams match on the 1/4" stitching line, so insert the pin at that spot. Insert the pins straight up and down rather than at an angle. When pinning the pieces together, pin them at each end. Then give a gentle stretch, holding on to each end, and pin in the middle. With a consistent 1/4" seam and accurate cutting, the seams will match with little effort.

Our general rule is to try to match a seam three times. If it still doesn't match, leave it and go on. You may choose to fix it later, or decide that it is close enough and continue.

PRESSING

It is necessary to press after each 45 Flip, Piggyback Flip, etc., so have a pressing pad and iron beside the sewing machine. Use the side of the iron when pressing, and press lightly. Heavy pressing can cause stretching and distortion. Press from the right side of the fabrics. This will prevent the small tuck that can change the size of the finished piece. Generally press toward the darker fabric, although some pieces will naturally press better in one direction than another. For better seam matching press seams in opposite directions.

TECHNIQUES

The techniques we use are good for us because we are not "mathematically inclined." It must be genetic! With our designs on graph paper, we see what must be accomplished and have tried to find the easiest way to get the desired result.

45 FLIP

The technique used most is the 45 Flip. A 45 Flip can be used on a square or rectangle base, and can be on any or all corners. Place a small square of fabric in the corner of the larger piece, right sides together, with raw edges even. Use a sharp pencil and ruler to draw a diagonal line from corner to corner across the small square. Stitch on drawn line. Trim, leaving a 1/4" seam allowance. Press from the top.

Half Inch Flips are small, 1" x 1", 45 Flips. These tiny flips give the illusion of roundness on feet or tails. For a rounder look, cut flips 3/4" x 3/4".

45 FLIPS IN ORDER

When sewing flips to a base piece, apply them in alphabetical order. The sewing order affects the design.

PIGGYBACK FLIP

Start with a 45 Flip. Place a smaller square on the corner of the completed 45 Flip; then repeat the technique for the 45 Flip. Use 45 Flips and Piggyback Flips on one, two, three, or all four corners of any square or rectangle.

45 JOINTS

With right sides together, make an "L" or reverse "L" with fabric rectangles. Draw a diagonal line as shown, and stitch. Trim, leaving a 1/4" seam allowance. This is the same technique we use to join strips for binding. It is wonderful, because you do not have to cut or sew unwieldy trapezoids.

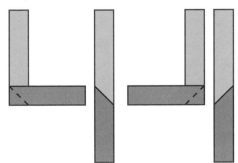

HALF RECTANGLE

Cut two rectangles the same size. Draw a diagonal line connecting opposite corners on the wrong side of one rectangle. Place the rectangles right sides together, matching corners, as shown. Stitch on the line. Trim, leaving 1/4" seam allowance. Press from the front out.

 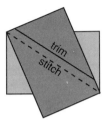

HALF RECTANGLE FLIP

On the wrong side of the piece to be flipped, mark 1/4" from upper right corner, and 1/4" from lower left corner as shown. Draw a stitching line from mark to mark (AC). Measure from A to B, and B to C. Mark the base piece with these same distances. Position flip piece on base as shown and stitch. Press outward from the front and trim.

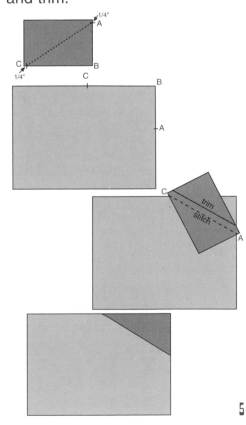

5

HALF STRIPS

Half Strips can be any size width and length to create the size piece you need. They can be horizontal or vertical depending on where they are used. For example: Cut a 1" x 4-1/2" piece of color #1 and a 1" x 4-1/2" piece of color #2. Sew together to make a 1-1/2" x 4-1/2" strip of fabric.

HALF STRIP FLIP

Use a square Half Strip to make a 45 Flip on another piece of fabric.

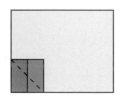 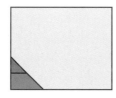

HALF SQUARE

Cut two squares the same size. Lay fabrics right sides together, matching grain line. Draw a diagonal line from corner to corner. Stitch, trim, and press.

HALF SQUARE FLIP

Use a Half Square for a 45 Flip.

TRIPLE FLIP

A Triple flip is a Half Square made with a Half Square and a square. Cut three squares the same size. Make a Half Square. Lay the remaining square on top of the Half Square. Stitch diagonally, trim, and press.

COMBINATION FLIP

The Combination Flip combines a large and small rectangle and a 45 Flip.

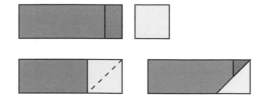

COUNTED PATCHWORK

We call our method "Counted Patchwork" because patterns are drawn on four squares per inch graph paper. The one inch grid allows you to see at a glance what size piece to cut. Add 1/2" for seam allowance to both the width and length of the piece. For example, if you COUNT 4", you will CUT 4-1/2" inches.

The Patterns are divided into Units (A, B, C, etc.) and the Units into numbered pieces. It is important to assemble the pieces in numeric order according to the assembly instructions.

We find it helpful to "pencil in" color choices so that you won't cut a piece from the wrong fabric. For example, Sheep Body (red pin dot), Sheep Face (gray floral), and so on. You can erase these later.

STRIP CUTTING

There is a strip cutting chart with each project. It tells how many strips to cut of each width, for each fabric. The numbered pieces are subcut from the strips. The subcutting chart indicates what width strip from which to cut. At times you will be able to cut more than one piece from a width of strip.

For example: Cut two 1-1/2" x 1-1/2" pieces next to each other from a 3-1/2" strip. Do not precut the whole Unit. We recommend subcutting only four or five pieces at a time, in numeric order.

DESIGN YOUR OWN

There are directions for each of the photographed quilts. You may want to combine animals differently, and we encourage you to do so. The Counted Patchwork method makes it easy to do.

There are a couple of ways to combine animals. The animals can be placed so that each one is within its own block, and you just pin blocks together. This is how Three Little Pigs was put together. You can also arrange the animals so that they merge. Yahoo and Barnyard Musicians are examples of animals merging in the quilt.

Copy the drawings of animals you want to use. Place them as you want them. If areas overlap draw this section on graph paper. Find dividing lines for Units; then divide the Units into pieces that will fit together, using 45 Flips and all the techniques where necessary. There is no "right" way, and not "one" way to divide. Sometimes there is a "better" way, which will eliminate extra pieces or give a smoother flow. Try it! Make sure that your pieces will fit together numerically in sections. Look at Unit D in the example at the top of the next page.

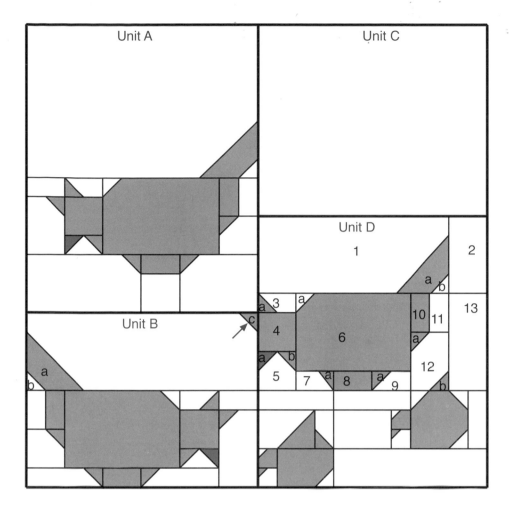

Unit A

Unit C

Unit D

1   2

a
b

3 a

a
c 4   6   10 11   13

a
5   7 a 8 a 9   12
a b
b

Unit B

a
b

First you would assemble pieces 1 and 2 of Unit D. Then assemble 3 through 5, 6 through 9, 10 through 12. Add 13, then join all the sections. In this simple example, see how piece #1 in the reversed hen, Unit B, will also have a piece #1c, indicated by the arrow, of the other hen? That is what we mean when we merge. In a complex design, you may have a piece with several different elements in it.

REVERSING THE IMAGE
Use graph paper to reverse an animal if you want it to face the opposite direction. As an example, let's reverse Hiss 'n' Fuss. Define a 12" x 12" area and draw a square. Pick a spot to begin. Draw three squares down, then diagonal down right one square, straight right one

square, diagonal up right one square, three squares up, diagonal down left one square, straight left one square, diagonal up left one square, and so on.

You can see how this is done by looking at the design on the graph paper, just count it out.

BORDERS AND BLOCKS
Wall hangings should hang flat and square, and we are becoming more willing to do everything we can to accomplish that. It helps to cut border strips on the lengthwise grain. Additional fabric may be needed for lengthwise strips.

Our pieced borders incorporate some easy, small blocks and simple combinations to create fun and interest. Borders should enhance the design, not detract from it.

The Delectable Mountains border used on Art and the Chickens created a sunrise effect. The method of piecing that border is one we learned from *Delectable Mountain Quilts, a New View* by Nancy Brenan Daniel.

Barnyard Musicians uses a print border. The designs are outline quilted, adding texture to the border.

Try using a striped fabric for a border. Quilt beside each stripe, giving the illusion that much work went into the border when it didn't.

Directions are given for all the blocks that are used in the borders and backgrounds, and we know that you will find and use a lot more.

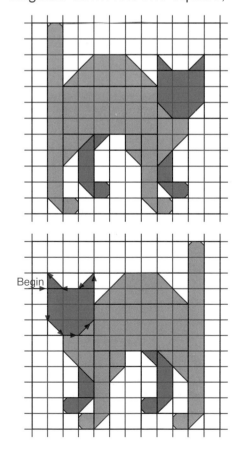

Begin

FINISHING TOUCHES

Mice need whiskers and tails,
  Chickens and geese need feet,
Kitties need whiskers and
  piggies need tails,
Now your quilt top's complete!

Hand or machine embroider these details once the top is complete, prior to layering and quilting.

MACHINE QUILTING

Our projects are machine quilted. Cut backing fabric and batting at least 2" larger than the top all the way around. Center the backing, wrong side up, on a table. We use a 36" x 72" table. Gently stretch and clamp the backing with binder clamps. Center the batting on top, being careful not to stretch it. Pat out any wrinkles or lumps; don't pull. Center and lay out the pieced top, right side is up. Carefully smooth onto batting.

Starting in the center, pin layers together with 1" safety pins. Gently smooth from the center out and pin every three or four inches.

Match the bobbin thread color to the backing. We match top thread colors to the quilt, changing as necessary. Clear monofilament can also be used. Outline the main elements of the design using a walking foot. Starting in the middle of the quilt, do the remaining quilting. Be sure to quilt as closely in the borders as in the body of the quilt. Remove all pins after the quilt is sufficiently quilted. Square the quilt before binding.

SLEEVES

To save time and hand stitching, we apply the sleeve after quilting is completed and before binding. Measure the width of the quilt, subtract 2". Cut 8-1/2" wide strips of sleeve fabric this measurement, sewing strips together if necessary. Sew a small double hem on each end of the sleeve strip. Fold and press in half lengthwise, wrong sides together. Match the center of the sleeve with the center of the top edge of the quilt on the back. Pin top and bottom of the sleeve in place. The top of the sleeve will be secured as the binding is sewn on, leaving only the bottom to be hand stitched.

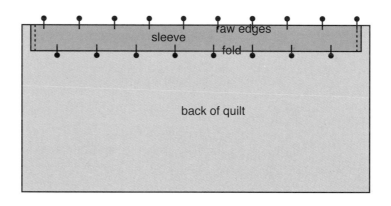

sleeve raw edges
fold

back of quilt

BINDING

We prefer a binding fabric that is different from any used in the body of the quilt. Usually, we use 2-1/2" cross-cut strips, joined with a 45 joint for the needed length, and pressed in half lengthwise. To figure the length of binding, measure all four sides then add 12" to the total.

Plaids and checks are interesting and charming, but look better when cut on the bias. Try not to apply a bias binding to a pieced border; it tends to stretch. Use a straight grain border for the final border when using bias binding.

Our barn was built at the turn of the century and burned in 1942. It was full of every size harness and saddles from Shetland to Belgian. The children played and daydreamed in the hayloft.

CODY AND HIS GIRLS
45" x 28"

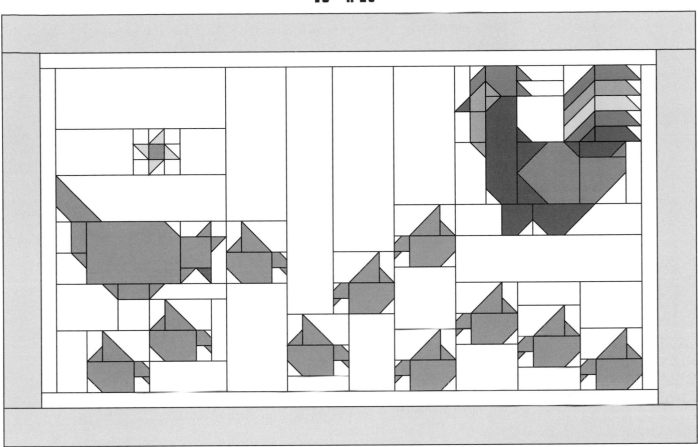

Designed by **Nancy Jewell**
Steamboat Springs, Colorado

YARDAGE

1-1/8 yds.	☐ Background
1/8 yd.	■ Rooster body
1/4 yd.	■ Rooster wing
Scraps	■ Comb
Scraps	■ Rooster face
Scraps	■ Feathers (assorted)
1/4 yd.	■ Hen
(3) 2-1/2" strips	■ Chicks (assorted)
3/8 yd.	☐ Border
1/3 yd.	Binding
1-1/2 yds.	Backing

CUTTING

Cut all strips crosswise as shown in Rotary Cutting. Cut the following strips, then refer to each Unit's cutting chart for size of pieces to cut from each strip. Pieces may be subcut from a wider strip.

Fabric		# of Strips	Strip Width
Background	☐	2	4-1/2"
		3	3-1/2"
		1	2-1/2"
		8	1-1/2"
Rooster body	■	1	2-1/2"
Rooster wing	■	1	4-1/2"
Hen	■	1	4-1/2"
Chicks	■	3 (assorted)	2-1/2"
Border	☐	4	3"

Do you remember hearing the chicks cheep in the post office, feed store, or depot? It was an exciting sound which meant that spring was here!

CHICKS

Make ten; six facing left, four facing right. Each 2-1/2" strip makes four chicks. Subcutting and directions are for one chick.

SUBCUTTING

Fabric	Strip Width	Pc #	Size
Background ☐	3-1/2"	1	3-1/2" x 2-1/2"
	1-1/2"	2	1-1/2" x 2-1/2"
		3a	1" x 1"
		4	1-1/2" x 1-1/2"
		5a	1-1/2" x 1-1/2"
Chick ■	2-1/2"	1a	2-1/2" x 2-1/2"
		2a	1-1/2" x 1-1/2"
		3	1-1/2" x 1-1/2"
		4a	1" x 1"
		5	3-1/2" x 2-1/2"

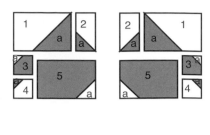

SEWING
1. 45 Flip - 1a, 2a, 3a, 4a, 5a.
2. Sew 1 thru 5 together as shown to complete each chick.

HEN & STAR - UNIT A

STAR SUBCUTTING

Fabric	Strip Width	Pc #	Size
Background ☐	1-1/2"	1, 2, 3, 4, 6, 7, 8, 9	1-1/2" x 1-1/2"
Border (star) ☐	3"	2, 4, 6, 8	1-1/2" x 1-1/2"
Chick (star center) ■	2-1/2"	5	1-1/2" x 1-1/2"

SEWING
1. 45 Flip a 1-1/2" background square to each 1-1/2" border square.
2. Sew 1 thru 9 together as shown to complete Star.

HEN SUBCUTTING

Fabric	Strip Width	Pc #	Size
Background ☐	4-1/2"	14	4-1/2" x 3-1/2"
		1	11-1/2" x 4-1/2"
	3-1/2"	4	11-1/2" x 3-1/2"
		2	5-1/2" x 3-1/2"
		3	3-1/2" x 3-1/2"
	2-1/2"	7	2-1/2" x 2-1/2"
		16	2-1/2" x 2-1/2"
		17	2-1/2" x 4-1/2"
		20	5-1/2" x 2-1/2"
	1-1/2"	4b	1-1/2" x 1-1/2"
		12	1-1/2" x 1-1/2"
		13	1-1/2" x 3-1/2"
		9	2-1/2" x 1-1/2"
		11	2-1/2" x 1-1/2"
		8a	1-1/2" x 1-1/2"
		5	1-1/2" x 2-1/2"
		18	5-1/2" x 1-1/2"
		19	1-1/2" x 4-1/2"

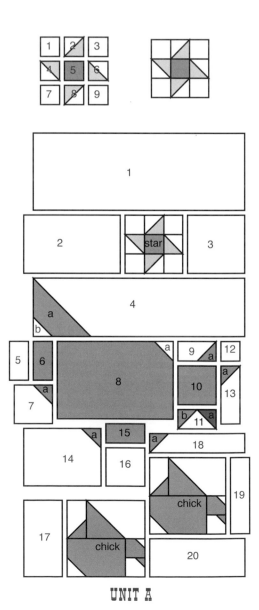

UNIT A

10

Subcutting, cont.

Fabric	Strip Width	Pc #	Size
Hen	4-1/2"	4a	3-1/2" x 3-1/2"
		13a	1-1/2" x 1-1/2"
		9a	1-1/2" x 1-1/2"
		10	2-1/2" x 2-1/2"
		11b	1-1/2" x 1-1/2"
		8	6-1/2" x 4-1/2"
		6	1-1/2" x 2-1/2"
		7a	1-1/2" x 1-1/2"
		18a	1-1/2" x 1-1/2"
		15	2-1/2" x 1-1/2"
		14a	1-1/2" x 1-1/2"
Chick (for beak)	2-1/2"	6a	1-1/2" x 1-1/2"

SEWING
1. 45 Flip - 4a, 7a, 8a, 9a, 11a, 11b, 13a, 14a, 18a.
2. Piggyback flip 4b.
3. Sew the star between 2 and 3. Add 1 on top.
4. Sew 4 thru 13 together as shown. Stitch below the Step 3 unit.
5. Sew 14 thru 16. Sew 17 to the left of a chick, stitch below 14-16.
6. Sew 19 to the right of a chick, stitch below 18. Add 20 below.
7. Sew the unit from Step 6 to the left of the unit from Step 5.
   Stitch this below the hen.

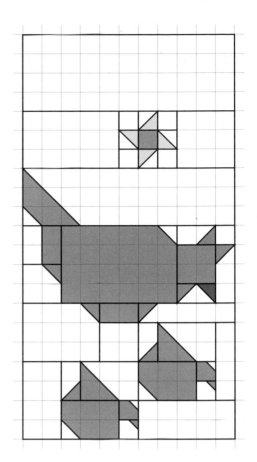

UNIT A

LOTS OF CHICKS - UNIT B
SUBCUTTING

Fabric	Strip Width	Pc #	Size
Background	4-1/2"	1	4-1/2" x 10-1/2"
		2	4-1/2" x 7-1/2"
		4	4-1/2" x 12-1/2"
		7	4-1/2" x 9-1/2"
		8	4-1/2" x 4-1/2"
	3-1/2"	6	3-1/2" x 5-1/2"
		3	3-1/2" x 16-1/2"
	1-1/2"	5	4-1/2" x 1-1/2"

SEWING

1. Sew five chicks and the pieces above together as shown to compete Unit B.

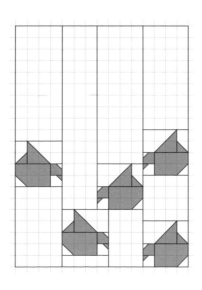

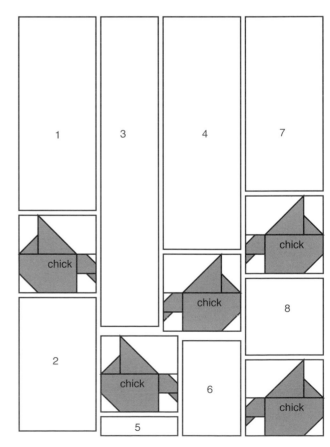

UNIT B

11

ROOSTER - UNIT C

SUBCUTTING

Fabric	Strip Width	Pc #	Size
Background	3-1/2"	11	3-1/2" x 3-1/2"
		24	3-1/2" x 2-1/2"
		28	12-1/2" x 3-1/2"
		29	4-1/2" x 3-1/2"
		32	4-1/2" x 3-1/2"
	2-1/2"	6	2-1/2" x 4-1/2"
		12a	2-1/2" x 2-1/2"
		22a	2-1/2" x 2-1/2"
		27	5-1/2" x 2-1/2"
		30	4-1/2" x 2"
		31	4-1/2" x 2"
	1-1/2"	1	1-1/2" x 3-1/2"
		2	1-1/2" x 2-1/2"
		3a	1-1/2" x 1-1/2"
		8b	1-1/2" x 1-1/2"
		9	3-1/2" x 1-1/2"
		10	3-1/2" x 1-1/2"
		15a	1-1/2" x 1-1/2"
		16a	1-1/2" x 1-1/2"
		17a	1-1/2" x 1-1/2"
		18a	1-1/2" x 1-1/2"
		19a	1-1/2" x 1-1/2"
		23	1-1/2" x 4-1/2"
		25a	1-1/2" x 1-1/2"
		26a	1-1/2" x 1-1/2"
Rooster body	2-1/2"	8	2-1/2" x 7-1/2"
		11a	1-1/2" x 1-1/2"
		20a,c	2-1/2" x 2-1/2"
		20b	1-1/2" x 1-1/2"
		21	3-1/2" x 1-1/2"
		25	2-1/2" x 2-1/2"
		26	4-1/2" x 2-1/2"
Rooster wing	4-1/2"	20	4-1/2" x 4-1/2"
		21a	1-1/2" x 1-1/2"
		22	3-1/2" x 3-1/2"

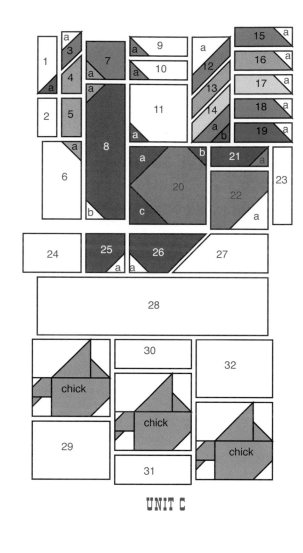

UNIT C

Use scraps for the remaining pieces. Pieces grouped together should be from the same fabric.

Fabric		Pc #	Size
Comb		3	1-1/2" x 2-1/2"
		7	2-1/2" x 2-1/2"
		9a	1-1/2" x 1-1/2"
		10a	1-1/2" x 1-1/2"
Rooster face		4	1-1/2" x 2-1/2"
		5	1-1/2" x 2-1/2"
		6a	1-1/2" x 1-1/2"
		7a	1-1/2" x 1-1/2"
		8a	1-1/2" x 1-1/2"

Cutting, cont.

Fabric		Pc #	Size
Feathers (assorted)	■	12	2-1/2" x 3-1/2"
		15	3-1/2" x 1-1/2"
		13	2-1/2" x 3-1/2"
		16	3-1/2" x 1-1/2"
		14	2-1/2" x 3-1/2"
		17	3-1/2" x 1-1/2"
		14a	2-1/2" x 2-1/2"
		18	3-1/2" x 1-1/2"
		14b	1-1/2" x 1-1/2"
		19	3-1/2" x 1-1/2"
Chick (for beak)	■	1a	1-1/2" x 1-1/2"

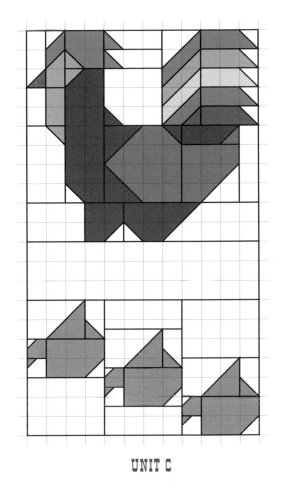

UNIT C

SEWING

1. 45 Flip - 1a, 3a, 6a, 7a, 8a, 8b, 9a, 10a, 11a, 12a, 15a, 16a, 17a, 18a, 19a, 20a, 20b, 20c, 21a, 22a, 25a, 26a.

2. Piggyback Flip - 14a, 14b.

3. 45 Joint - 3 to 4, 12 to 13 to 14, 26 to 27.

4. Sew 1 thru 28 together as shown to complete the rooster.

5. Sew three chicks and pieces 29 - 32 together as shown. Stitch this below the rooster.

ASSEMBLY

1. Sew Units A, B, and C together.
2. Sew 1-1/2" background strips to all four sides.
3. Sew 3" border strips to all four sides.

DETAILS

1. Embroider feet on the rooster, hen, and chicks.
2. Make French knots for eyes on the chicks.
3. Quilt feathers on the rooster, hen, and chicks.
4. Nancy quilted a fence in the background.

Our family raised 50 chickens a year, from chick to fryer, and eggs in between. Nothing compares to Great Grandma's home raised fried chickens!

TICK TALK
48" x 36"

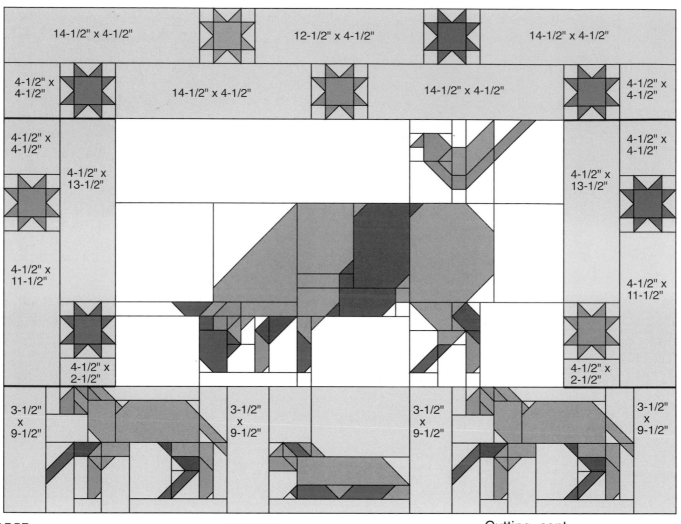

YARDAGE

3/4 yd.	☐	Background
1/4 yd.	☐	Sheep body
1/4 yd.	☐	Sheep center body
1/8 yd.	☐	Sheep face
1/8 yd.	☐	Sheep ear & far feet
1/4 yd. *	☐	Lamb body
1/4 yd. *	☐	Lamb far legs
1/4 yd. *	☐	Lamb face
1/8 yd.	☐	Bird body
1/8 yd.	☐	Bird wing
1-1/3 yds.	☐	Border
5 - 2-1/2" strips	☐	Stars (assorted)
1/2 yd.		Binding
1-1/2 yds.		Backing

* Make the lambs as shown or mix the fabrics for more variety.

CUTTING

Cut all strips crosswise as shown in Rotary Cutting. Cut the following strips, then refer to each Unit's cutting chart for size of pieces to cut from each strip. Pieces may be subcut from a wider strip.

Fabric		# of Strips	Strip Width
Background	☐	1	7-1/2"
		1	6-1/2"
		1	2-1/2"
		1	1-1/2"
Sheep body	☐	1	6-1/2"
Sheep center body	☐	1	4-1/2"
Sheep face	☐	1	2-1/2"

Cutting, cont.

Fabric		# of Strips	Strip Width
Sheep ear & far feet	☐	1	2-1/2"
Lamb body	☐	2	3-1/2"
Lamb far legs	☐	1	2-1/2"
Lamb face	☐	1	2-1/2"
Bird body	☐	1	3-1/2"
Bird wing	☐	1	2-1/2"
Border	☐	1	5-1/2"
		4	4-1/2"
		1	3-1/2"
		3	2-1/2"
		3	1-1/2"
Stars (assorted)	☐	5	2-1/2"

14

MAGPIE - UNIT A

SUBCUTTING

Fabric		Strip Width	Pc #	Size
Background	☐	7-1/2"	5	3-1/2" x 3-1/2"
			12	2-1/2" x 3-1/2"
		6-1/2"	13	5-1/2" x 6-1/2"
			14	21-1/2" x 6-1/2"
		2-1/2"	1	3-1/2" x 1-1/2"
			6	1-1/2" x 2-1/2"
			10a	2-1/2" x 2-1/2"
			13b	2-1/2" x 2-1/2"
		1-1/2"	2a	1-1/2" x 1-1/2"
			3	1-1/2" x 1-1/2"
			4a	1-1/2" x 1-1/2"
			9	1-1/2" x 1-1/2"
Bird body	▨	3-1/2"	2	1-1/2" x 1-1/2"
			4	2-1/2" x 2-1/2"
			5a	2-1/2" x 2-1/2"
			8	1-1/2" x 1-1/2"
			11	2-1/2" x 3-1/2"
			13a	3-1/2" x 3-1/2"
Bird wing	▨	2-1/2"	4b	1-1/2" x 1-1/2"
			5b	1-1/2" x 1-1/2"
			7	1-1/2" x 2-1/2"
			10	2-1/2" x 4-1/2"

If you weren't very big, and turned your back on a bum lamb, you were sure to get butted and knocked down!

SEWING

1. 45 Flip - 2a, 4a, 4b, 10a.
2. Piggyback Flip - 5a, 5b, 13a, 13b.
3. 45 Joint - 10 to 11 to 12.
4. Sew 1 thru 14 together as shown to complete Unit A.

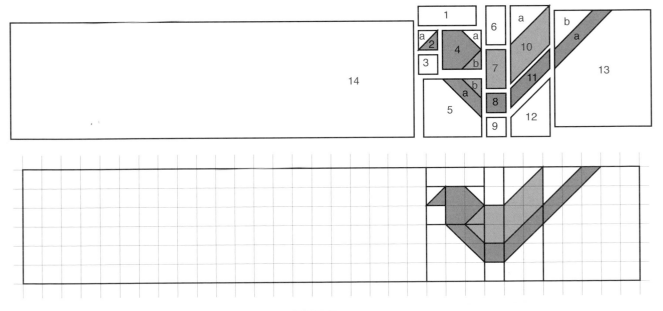

UNIT A

SHEEP HEAD - UNIT B

SUBCUTTING

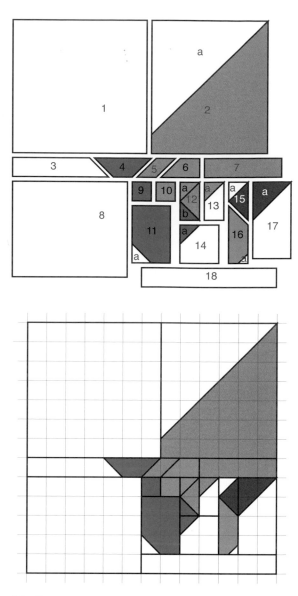

Fabric		Strip Width	Pc #	Size
Background	☐	7-1/2"	1	7-1/2" x 7-1/2"
			2a	6-1/2" x 6-1/2"
			17	2-1/2" x 4-1/2"
		6-1/2"	8	6-1/2" x 5-1/2"
		2-1/2"	13	1-1/2" x 2-1/2"
			14	2-1/2" x 2-1/2"
		1-1/2"	3	5-1/2" x 1-1/2"
			11a	1-1/2" x 1-1/2"
			15a	1-1/2" x 1-1/2"
			16a	1" x 1"
			18	7-1/2" x 1-1/2"
Sheep body	▨	6-1/2"	2	6-1/2" x 7-1/2"
			5	2-1/2" x 1-1/2"
			7	4-1/2" x 1-1/2"
			12	1-1/2" x 2-1/2"
			13a	1-1/2" x 1-1/2"
Sheep center body	■	4-1/2"	15	1-1/2" x 2-1/2"
			17a	2-1/2" x 2-1/2"
Sheep face	▨	2-1/2"	4	3-1/2" x 1-1/2"
			9	1-1/2" x 1-1/2"
			11	2-1/2" x 3-1/2"
			12b	1-1/2" x 1-1/2"
			14a	1-1/2" x 1-1/2"
Sheep ear & far feet	▨	2-1/2"	6	2-1/2" x 1-1/2"
			10	1-1/2" x 1-1/2"
			12a	1-1/2" x 1-1/2"
			16	1-1/2" x 3-1/2"

UNIT B

SEWING

1. 45 Flip - 2a, 11a, 12a, 12b, 13a, 14a, 15a, 16a, 17a.

2. 45 Joint - 3 to 4 to 5 to 6, 15 to 16.

3. Sew 1 thru 18 together as shown to complete Unit B.

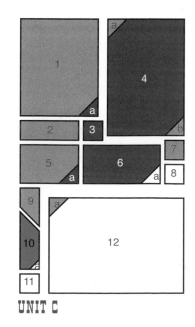

UNIT C

CENTER SHEEP - UNIT C

SUBCUTTING

Fabric	Strip Width	Pc #	Size
Background ☐	7-1/2"	12	7-1/2" x 5-1/2"
	1-1/2"	6a	1-1/2" x 1-1/2"
		8	1-1/2" x 1-1/2"
		10a	1" x 1"
		11	1-1/2" x 1-1/2"
Sheep body ▨	6-1/2"	1	4-1/2" x 5-1/2"
		2	3-1/2" x 1-1/2"
		4a,b	1-1/2" x 1-1/2"
		5	3-1/2" x 2-1/2"
		7	1-1/2" x 1-1/2"
		9	1-1/2" x 2-1/2"
		12a	1-1/2" x 1-1/2"
Sheep center body ▪	4-1/2"	1a	1-1/2" x 1-1/2"
		3	1-1/2" x 1-1/2"
		4	4-1/2" x 6-1/2"
		5a	1-1/2" x 1-1/2"
		6	4-1/2" x 2-1/2"
Sheep face ▪	2-1/2"	10	1-1/2" x 3-1/2"

SEWING

1. 45 Flip - 1a, 4a, 4b, 5a, 6a, 10a, 12a.
2. 45 Joint - 9 to 10.
3. Sew 1 thru 12 together as shown to complete Unit C.

SHEEP RUMP - UNIT D

SUBCUTTING

Fabric	Strip Width	Pc #	Size
Background ☐	7-1/2"	2	5-1/2" x 7-1/2"
		5	2-1/2" x 3-1/2"
		8	2-1/2" x 3-1/2"
	6-1/2"	11	6-1/2" x 6-1/2"
	2-1/2"	1b,c	2-1/2" x 2-1/2"
		3a	2-1/2" x 2-1/2"
		6	2-1/2" x 1-1/2"
	1-1/2"	4b	1-1/2" x 1-1/2"
		5b	1-1/2" x 1-1/2"
		7a	1-1/2" x 1-1/2"
		10	1-1/2" x 1-1/2"
		9b	1" x 1"
Sheep body ▨	6-1/2"	1	6-1/2" x 7-1/2"
		3	3-1/2" x 2-1/2"
		4a,c	1-1/2" x 1-1/2"
		7	2-1/2" x 1-1/2"
Sheep center body ▪	4-1/2"	1a	1-1/2" x 1-1/2"
		4	2-1/2" x 2-1/2"
		9a	1-1/2" x 1-1/2"
Sheep face ▪	2-1/2"	5a	2-1/2" x 2-1/2"
		8a	1-1/2" x 1-1/2"
Sheep ear & far feet ▨	2-1/2"	9	1-1/2" x 3-1/2"

SEWING

1. 45 Flip - 1a, 1b, 1c, 3a, 4a, 4b, 4c, 7a, 8a, 9a, 9b.
2. Piggyback Flip - 5a, 5b.
3. Sew 1 thru 11 together as shown to complete Unit D.

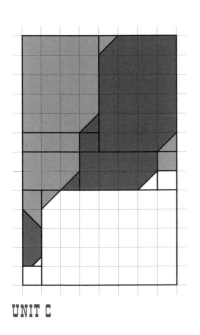

UNIT C

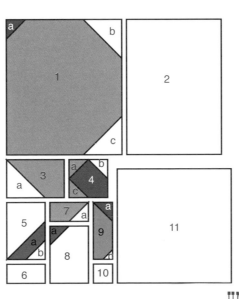

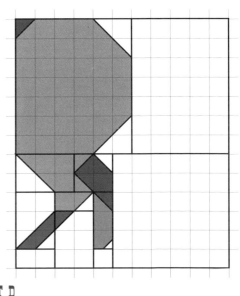

UNIT D

STANDING LAMB

This lamb is made twice. The pieces listed below are for one lamb.

SUBCUTTING

Fabric		Strip Width	Pc #	Size
Border	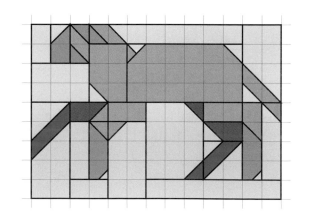 (light swatch)	5-1/2"	4	3-1/2" x 2-1/2"
			9	2-1/2" x 4-1/2"
			10a	2-1/2" x 2-1/2"
			11	2-1/2" x 4-1/2"
			18	3-1/2" x 4-1/2"
		2-1/2"	1	1-1/2" x 2-1/2"
			6	7-1/2" x 1-1/2"
			13	1-1/2" x 3-1/2"
			15	2-1/2" x 1-1/2"
			17	2-1/2" x 4-1/2"
			21	2-1/2" x 2-1/2"
			24	1-1/2" x 4-1/2"
		1-1/2"	2a	1-1/2" x 1-1/2"
			7a	1-1/2" x 1-1/2"
			8b,c	1-1/2" x 1-1/2"
			9b	1-1/2" x 1-1/2"
			14b	1" x 1"
			20a	1-1/2" x 1-1/2"
			21b	1-1/2" x 1-1/2"
			23a	1" x 1"
			25	7-1/2" x 1-1/2"
Sheep center body	(dark swatch)	4-1/2"	12	2-1/2" x 1-1/2"
			18a	1-1/2" x 1-1/2"
			20	2-1/2" x 1-1/2"
Lamb body	(light swatch)	3-1/2"	3	1-1/2" x 2-1/2"
			5	2-1/2" x 1-1/2"
			7	2-1/2" x 3-1/2"
			8	6-1/2" x 3-1/2"
			8a	1-1/2" x 1-1/2"
			9a	2-1/2" x 2-1/2"
			12a	1-1/2" x 1-1/2"
			14a	1-1/2" x 1-1/2"
			16	2-1/2" x 1-1/2"
			17a	1-1/2" x 1-1/2"
			19	2-1/2" x 1-1/2"
			22	1-1/2" x 2-1/2"
			24a	1-1/2" x 1-1/2"
Lamb far legs	(dark swatch)	2-1/2"	10	2-1/2" x 3-1/2"
			18b	1-1/2" x 1-1/2"
			21a	2-1/2" x 2-1/2"
Lamb face	(swatch)	2-1/2"	2	1-1/2" x 2-1/2"
			3a	1-1/2" x 1-1/2"
			3b	1-1/2" x 1-1/2"
			5a	1-1/2" x 1-1/2"
			14	1-1/2" x 3-1/2"
			23	1-1/2" x 3-1/2"

SEWING

1. Half Square Flip - Make a half square with 8a and 8b. Flip it on 8.

2. 45 Flip - 2a, 3a, 3b, 5a, 7a, 8c, 10a, 12a, 14a, 14b, 17a, 18a, 18b, 20a, 23a, 24a.

3. Piggyback Flip - 9a, 9b, 21a, 21b.

4. 45 Joint - 5 to 6, 10 to 11, 22 to 23.

5. Sew 1 thru 25 together as shown to complete the standing lamb.

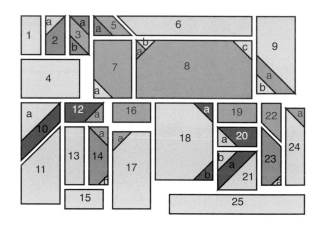

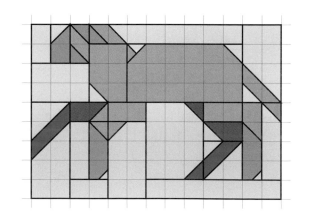

LYING DOWN LAMB

SUBCUTTING

Fabric		Strip Width	Pc #	Size
Border	▢	5-1/2"	1	3-1/2" x 4-1/2"
			4	7-1/2" x 5-1/2"
		2-1/2"	6	2-1/2" x 2-1/2"
			7a	2-1/2" x 2-1/2"
		1-1/2"	2a	1-1/2" x 1-1/2"
			6a	1-1/2" x 1-1/2"
			12	10-1/2" x 1-1/2"
Lamb body	▢	3-1/2"	3a,b	1-1/2" x 1-1/2"
			4a	1-1/2" x 1-1/2"
			5a	1-1/2" x 1-1/2"
			7	8-1/2" x 2-1/2"
			9	2-1/2" x 1-1/2"
			11	2-1/2" x 1-1/2"
Lamb far legs		2-1/2"	3	2-1/2" x 1-1/2"
	▪		6b	1-1/2" x 1-1/2"
			8	3-1/2" x 1-1/2"
			10	4-1/2" x 1-1/2"
Lamb face	▢	2-1/2"	2	1-1/2" x 1-1/2"
			5	2-1/2" x 1-1/2"

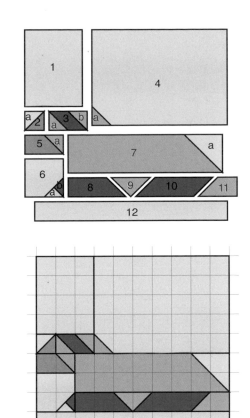

SEWING

1. Half Square Flip - Make a half square with 6a and 6b. Flip to 6.
2. 45 Flip - 2a, 3a, 3b, 4a, 5a, 7a.
3. 45 Joint - 8 to 9 to 10 to 11.
4. Sew 1 thru 12 together as shown to complete the lying down lamb.

BORDER SUBCUTTING

Fabric		Strip Width	# to Cut	Size
Border	▢	4-1/2"	4	14-1/2" x 4-1/2"
			4	4-1/2" x 4-1/2"
			1	12-1/2" x 4-1/2"
			2	4-1/2" x 13-1/2"
			2	4-1/2" x 11-1/2"
			2	4-1/2" x 2-1/2"
		3-1/2"	4	3-1/2" x 9-1/2"
		2-1/2"	36	2-1/2" x 1-1/2"
		1-1/2"	36	1-1/2" x 1-1/2"
Star	▪	2-1/2"	9	2-1/2" x 2-1/2" (2 per strip)
			72	1-1/2" x 1-1/2" (16 per strip)

STAR BLOCKS

1. 45 Flip a 1-1/2" Star square to both ends of each 2-1/2" x 1-1/2" Border.
2. Assemble nine stars as shown using a 2-1/2" Star square, four units from Step 1, and four 1-1/2" Border squares for each star.

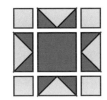

ASSEMBLY

1. Sew Units B, C, and D together. Add Unit A on top.
2. Make two side borders as shown in the diagram on page 14. Use the pieces cut above, and the stars. Sew these to the sides of the sheep.
3. Sew the lambs together in a row with 3-1/2" x 9-1/2" Border pieces between and on the ends. Sew this below the sheep.
4. Sew a top border as shown on page 14. Use the pieces cut above, and the stars. Sew this to the top of the sheep to complete the quilt top.

ART AND THE CHICKENS
55" x 45"

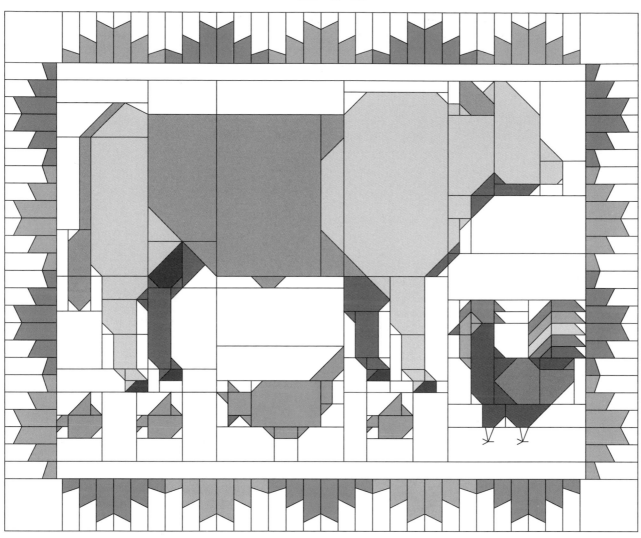

YARDAGE

2-1/8 yds.	☐ Background
5/8 yd.	☐ Bull head, rump & shoulder
3/8 yd.	☐ Bull body
1/4 yd.	☐ Bull far legs
1/8 yd.	■ Bull hooves
1/8 yd.	■ Rooster body
1/4 yd.	■ Rooster wing
Scraps	Feathers (assorted)
1/4 yd.	☐ Hen
1/8 yd.	☐ Chicks
3/8 yd.	☐ Border 1
3/8 yd.	☐ Border 2
1/2 yd.	Binding
2-7/8 yds.	Backing

CUTTING

Cut all strips crosswise as shown in Rotary Cutting. Cut the following strips, then refer to each Unit's cutting chart for size of pieces to cut from each strip. Pieces may be subcut from a wider strip.

Fabric		# of Strips	Strip Width
Background	☐	1	12-1/2"
		4	3-1/2"
		3	2-1/2"
		3	2"
		3	1-1/2"
Bull head, rump & shoulder	☐	1	9-1/2"
		1	4-1/2"
		1	2-1/2"

Cutting, cont.

Fabric		# of Strips	Strip Width
Bull body	☐	1	9-1/2"
		1	2-1/2"
Bull far legs	■	1	4-1/2"
Bull hooves	■	1	3-1/2"
Rooster body	■	1	2-1/2"
Rooster wing	■	1	4-1/2"
Hen	☐	1	4-1/2"
Chicks	■	1	2-1/2"

ROOSTER, HEN, CHICKS

Make a rooster, hen, and three chicks as explained on pages 10-13. The chicks use one 2-1/2" background strip and one 2-1/2" chick strip. The hen uses one 3-1/2" background strip, one 4-1/2" hen strip, and chick strips for the beak. Eliminate pieces 1-3, the star, 17, 19-20, and the chicks in piecing. Substitute a 5-1/2" x 3-1/2" background for piece #18.

The rooster uses a 1-1/2" and a 3-1/2" background strips, a 2-1/2" rooster body strip, a 4-1/2" rooster wing strip, and scraps for the feathers, comb, face, and beak. Use only pieces 1-28.

BULL - UNIT A
SUBCUTTING

Fabric		Strip Width	Pc #	Size
Background		12-1/2"	13	4-1/2" x 5-1/2"
	☐	3-1/2"	2	5-1/2" x 3-1/2"
			10	1-1/2" x 3-1/2"
			12	1-1/2" x 3-1/2"
			16	1-1/2" x 3-1/2"
			17	1-1/2" x 3-1/2"
			19	1-1/2" x 3-1/2"
		2-1/2"	1	8-1/2" x 2-1/2"
			4a	2-1/2" x 1-1/2"
			5	2-1/2" x 8-1/2"
			7	1-1/2" x 4-1/2"
			8a	1-1/2" x 1-1/2"
			9a	1-1/2" x 1-1/2"
			11a,b	1-1/2" x 1-1/2"
			15a	1-1/2" x 1-1/2"
			20	6-1/2" x 2-1/2"
			21a	1-1/2" x 1-1/2"
Bull head, rump & shoulder	▢	9-1/2"	4	5-1/2" x 3-1/2"
			9	5-1/2" x 12-1/2"
		4-1/2"	14	4-1/2" x 2-1/2"
			15	3-1/2" x 3-1/2"
			18	2-1/2" x 3-1/2"
		2-1/2"	20a	1-1/2" x 1-1/2"
			21	2-1/2" x 1-1/2"
			22a	1-1/2" x 1-1/2"
Bull body	▨	9-1/2"	3	4-1/2" x 3-1/2"
			6	1-1/2" x 8-1/2"
			8	2-1/2" x 4-1/2"
		2-1/2"	11	2-1/2" x 3-1/2"
Bull far legs	▪	4-1/2"	14a	1-1/2" x 1-1/2"
			16a	1-1/2" x 1-1/2"
Bull hooves	▪	3-1/2"	22	2-1/2" x 1-1/2"

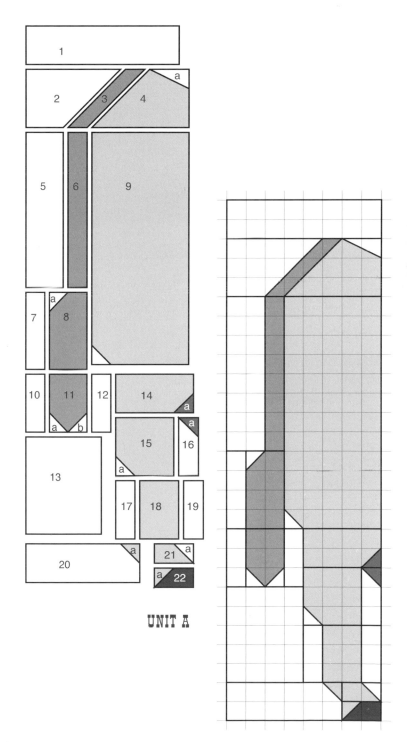

UNIT A

SEWING
1. 45 Flip - 8a, 9a, 11a, 11b, 14a, 15a, 16a, 20a, 21a, 22a.
2. 45 Joint - 2 to 3 to 4.
3. Rectangle Flip - 4a.
4. Sew 1 thru 22 together as shown to complete Unit A.

BULL - UNIT B

SUBCUTTING

Fabric	Strip Width	Pc #	Size
Background	12-1/2"	6	4-1/2" x 7-1/2" (cut next to piece 7 of Unit E)
	3-1/2"	1	6-1/2" x 3-1/2"
		4a	3-1/2" x 3-1/2"
		10	3-1/2" x 2-1/2"
	2-1/2"	5a	1-1/2" x 1-1/2"
		7	1-1/2" x 2-1/2"
		9	2-1/2" x 1-1/2"
Bull head, rump & shoulder	4-1/2"	2a	3-1/2" x 3-1/2"
		3a	3-1/2" x 3-1/2"
Bull body	9-1/2"	2	6-1/2" x 11-1/2"
		4b	3-1/2" x 3-1/2"
Bull far legs	4-1/2"	3b,c	1-1/2" x 1-1/2"
		4	3-1/2" x 4-1/2"
		5	2-1/2" x 7-1/2"
		6a,b	1-1/2" x 1-1/2"
		8a	1-1/2" x 1-1/2"
Bull hooves	3-1/2"	3	3-1/2" x 4-1/2"
		8	2-1/2" x 1-1/2"

SEWING
1. 45 Flip - 2a, 3a, 3b, 3c, 5a, 6a, 6b, 8a.
2. Flips in Order - 4a, 4b.
3. Sew 1 thru 10 together as shown to complete Unit B.

BULL - UNIT C

SUBCUTTING

Fabric	Strip Width	Pc #	Size
Background	12-1/2"	9	11-1/2" x 5-1/2"
	3-1/2"	1	11-1/2" x 3-1/2"
	2-1/2"	6	4-1/2" x 1-1/2"
	1-1/2"	8	6-1/2" x 1-1/2"
Bull head, rump, & shoulder	2-1/2"	4	2-1/2" x 10-1/2"
Bull body	9-1/2"	2	9-1/2" x 14-1/2"
	2-1/2"	3	2-1/2" x 4-1/2"
		5	2-1/2" x 4-1/2"
		7	3-1/2" x 1-1/2"

SEWING
1. 45 Joint - 3 to 4 to 5, 6 to 7 to 8.
2. Sew 1 thru 9 together as shown to complete Unit C.

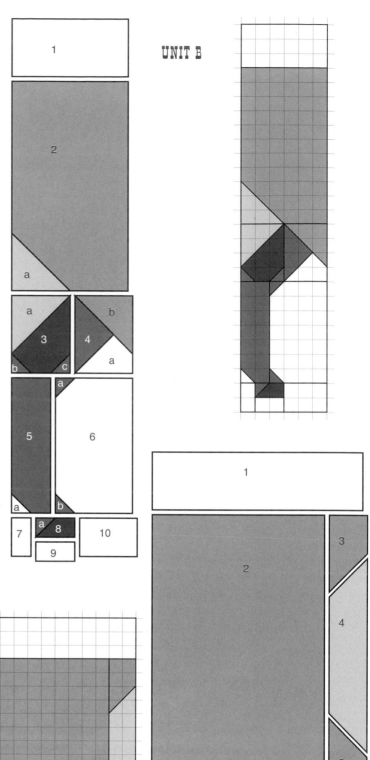

UNIT B

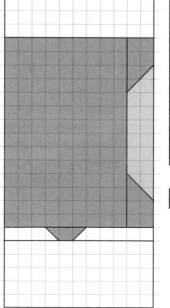

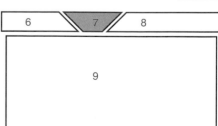

UNIT C

22

BULL - UNIT D

SUBCUTTING

Fabric		Strip Width	Pc #	Size
Background	☐	3-1/2"	2a	2-1/2" x 2-1/2"
			7	2-1/2" x 3-1/2"
		2-1/2"	10	2-1/2" x 1-1/2"
			15	2-1/2" x 9-1/2"
			16	2-1/2" x 1-1/2"
		1-1/2"	1	9-1/2" x 1-1/2"
			2d,e	1-1/2" x 1-1/2"
			3b	1-1/2" x 1-1/2"
			4	1-1/2" x 4-1/2"
			6	1-1/2" x 4-1/2"
			8a	1-1/2" x 1-1/2"
			11a	1-1/2" x 1-1/2"
			12	1-1/2" x 4-1/2"
			14a	1-1/2" x 1-1/2"
			18	1-1/2" x 1-1/2"
Bull head, rump & shoulder	▢	9-1/2"	2	9-1/2" x 16-1/2"
		4-1/2"	3a	2-1/2" x 2-1/2"
			11	3-1/2" x 5-1/2"
			13	2-1/2" x 3-1/2"
		2-1/2"	14	2-1/2" x 1-1/2"
			15a	1-1/2" x 1-1/2"
			17a	1-1/2" x 1-1/2"
Bull body	▨	2-1/2"	2b	2-1/2" x 2-1/2"
Bull far legs	▩	4-1/2"	2c	2-1/2" x 2-1/2"
			3	4-1/2" x 3-1/2"
			4a	1-1/2" x 1-1/2"
			5	2-1/2" x 4-1/2"
			7a	1-1/2" x 1-1/2"
			8	2-1/2" x 1-1/2"
			9a	1-1/2" x 1-1/2"
Bull hooves	■	3-1/2"	9	2-1/2" x 1-1/2"
			17	2-1/2" x 1-1/2"

SEWING

1. 45 Flip - 2a, 2b, 2e, 3a, 3b, 4a, 7a, 8a, 9a, 11a, 14a, 15a, 17a.

2. Piggyback Flip - 2c, 2d.

3. Sew 1 thru 18 together as shown to complete Unit D.

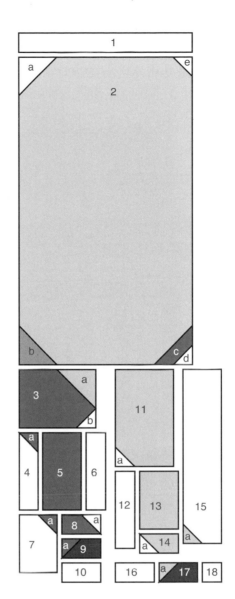

UNIT D

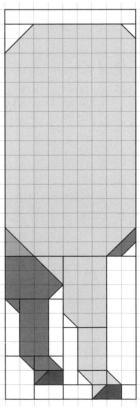

23

BULL - UNIT E

SUBCUTTING

Fabric	Strip Width	Pc #	Size
Background ☐	12-1/2"	7	4-1/2" x 7-1/2"
			(cut next to
			piece 6, Unit B)
		14	10-1/2" x 5-1/2"
		15	12-1/2" x 4-1/2"
	3-1/2"	3b	2-1/2" x 2-1/2"
		5a	3-1/2" x 3-1/2"
		10	2-1/2" x 3-1/2"
		13	1-1/2" x 3-1/2"
	2-1/2"	1	1-1/2" x 2-1/2"
		9	2-1/2" x 1-1/2"
	1-1/2"	6a	1-1/2" x 1-1/2"
		8a	1" x 1"
Bull head, rump, & shoulder	9-1/2"	5	4-1/2" x 9-1/2"
	4-1/2"	3a	2-1/2" x 2-1/2"
		4	4-1/2" x 7-1/2"
	2-1/2"	2	1-1/2" x 1-1/2"
		3c	1-1/2" x 1-1/2"
		7a	2-1/2" x 2-1/2"
		8	2-1/2" x 2-1/2"
		11	2-1/2" x 2-1/2"
		12	1-1/2" x 3-1/2"
		13a	1-1/2" x 1-1/2"
Bull body ▦	9-1/2"	3	3-1/2" x 3-1/2"
Bull far legs ▦	4-1/2"	4a	2-1/2" x 2-1/2"
		5b	1-1/2" x 1-1/2"
		6	4-1/2" x 1-1/2"
		12a	1-1/2" x 1-1/2"
		14a	2-1/2" x 2-1/2"
		15a	1-1/2" x 1-1/2"

UNIT E

SEWING

1. 45 Flip - 3c, 4a, 5a, 5b, 6a, 7a, 8a, 12a, 13a, 14a, 15a.
2. Half Square Flip - 3a and 3b.
3. Sew 1 thru 15 together as shown to complete Unit E.

ASSEMBLY

Subcutting

Fabric	Strip Width	# to Cut	Size
Background ☐	3-1/2"	3	3-1/2" x 6-1/2"
		1	2-1/2" x 6-1/2"
	2-1/2"	3	4-1/2" x 2-1/2"

1. Sew a 4-1/2" x 2-1/2" background below each chick.
2. Sew together a chick unit, a 3-1/2" x 6-1/2" background, a chick unit, a 3-1/2" x 6-1/2" background.
3. Sew Units A and B together. Add the unit made in Step 2 below AB.
4. Sew the hen below Unit C. Sew this to AB.
5. Sew together a 2-1/2" x 6-1/2" background, a chick unit, a 3-1/2" x 6-1/2" background. Sew this below Unit D. Add this to ABC.
6. Sew the rooster below Unit E. Sew this to ABCD.
7. Sew 2" strips to the top and bottom of the quilt.

DELECTABLE MOUNTAIN BORDER

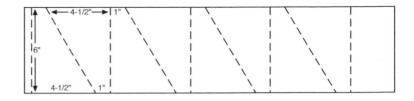

Cutting

Fabric	# of Strips	Strip Width
Background	4	6"
Border 1	2	6"
Border 2	2	6"

1. Cut one 5-1/2" x 5" piece from the end of each background strip.

2. Lay two 6" background strips right sides together.

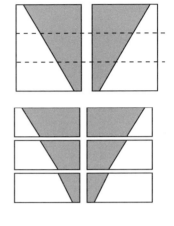

3. Cut as shown at right. The strips must be right sides together to get reverse pieces. Repeat with remaining background strips. Cut 18 and 18 reverse.

4. Use two 6" Border 1 strips and repeat Steps 2 and 3. Cut 9 and 9 reverse.

5. Repeat Steps 2 and 3 with two 6" Border 2 strips. Cut 9 and 9 reverse.

6. Sew each background piece to a border piece the same shape.

7. Sew each reverse background piece to a border piece the same shape.

8. Cut these units into 2" segments.

9. Sew the segments from a unit and reverse unit together to make a Border Unit. Use all Border 1 fabric or all Border 2 fabric in each unit. Make 9 units of each fabric.

10. Sew two rows of four Border Units, alternating Border 1 and Border 2 Units. Begin one with Border 1 and one with Border 2. Stitch these to the sides of the quilt.

11. Sew two rows of five Border Units, again alternating colors. Add a 5-1/2" x 5" background square to the ends of each row. Sew these to the top and bottom of the quilt.

The boys rode a big old gentle Hereford bull all around the farm. His name was Fred. He must have liked kids!

BARNYARD BUDDIES
48" x 40"

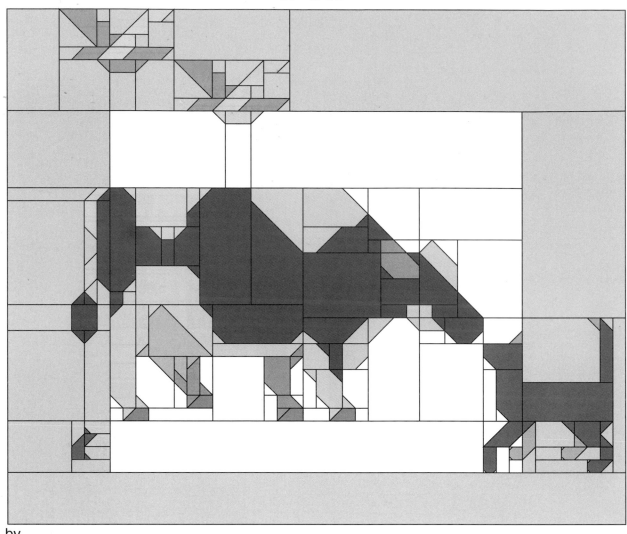

Designed by
Kathy Brunskill Faucett
Hayden, Colorado

YARDAGE

3/4 yd.		Background
1/3 yd.		Cow body & face
1/8 yd.		Cow ear & far legs
1/3 yd.		Cow belly, back, & near legs
1/4 yd.		Udder
1/8 yd.		Bird body
1/8 yd.		Bird wing
1/8 yd.		Cat body
1/8 yd.		Cat far legs
Scrap		Hooves
Scrap		Mouse
1 yd.		Border
1/2 yd.		Binding
2-5/8 yds.		Backing

CUTTING

Cut all strips crosswise as shown in Rotary Cutting. Cut the following strips, then refer to each Unit's cutting chart for size of pieces to cut from each strip. Pieces may be subcut from a wider strip.

Fabric		# of Strips	Strip Width
Background		2	6-1/2"
		2	4-1/2"
		1	1-1/2"
Cow body & face		1	5-1/2"
		1	2-1/2"
		1	1-1/2"
Cow ear & far legs		1	2-1/2"

Cutting, cont.

Fabric		# of Strips	Strip Width
Cow belly back, & legs		1	4-1/2"
		1	2-1/2"
		1	1-1/2"
Udder		1	4-1/2"
Bird body		1	3-1/2"
Bird wing		1	2-1/2"
Cat body		1	3-1/2"
Cat far legs		1	1-1/2"
Border		2	8-1/2"
		2	4-1/2"
		1	2-1/2"
		1	1-1/2"

UNIT A

SUBCUTTING

Fabric		Strip Width	Pc #	Size
Background	☐	6-1/2"	1	9-1/2" x 6-1/2"
			3	2-1/2" x 5-1/2"
			4	21-1/2" x 6-1/2"
Bird body	▨	3-1/2"	1a	1-1/2" x 1-1/2"
			2	2-1/2" x 1-1/2"
			4a	1-1/2" x 1-1/2"

SEWING

1. 45 Flip - 1a, 4a

2. Sew 1 thru 4 together as shown to complete Unit A.

UNIT A

COW - UNIT B

SUBCUTTING

Fabric		Strip Width	Pc #	Size
Cow body & face	▨	5-1/2"	12	4-1/2" x 9-1/2"
			14	4-1/2" x 8-1/2"
		2-1/2"	1	2-1/2" x 8-1/2"
			6	1-1/2" x 2-1/2"
			7	2-1/2" x 3-1/2"
			9	1-1/2" x 2-1/2"
			10	2-1/2" x 3-1/2"
		1-1/2"	2	1-1/2" x 1-1/2"
			11a	1-1/2" x 1-1/2"
Cow belly, back & near legs	☐	4-1/2"	4	4-1/2" x 3-1/2"
			11	5-1/2" x 3-1/2"
			13	4-1/2" x 5-1/2"
		2-1/2"	5	1-1/2" x 2-1/2"
		1-1/2"	1a,b	1-1/2" x 1-1/2"
			3	1-1/2" x 1-1/2"
			7a	1-1/2" x 1-1/2"
			8	1-1/2" x 1-1/2"
			10a	1-1/2" x 1-1/2"
			12a	1-1/2" x 1-1/2"

SEWING

1. 45 Flip - 1a, 1b, 7a, 10a, 11a 12a.
2. 45 Joint - 5 to 6 and 13 to 14.
3. Sew 1 thru 14 together as shown to complete Unit B.

UNIT B

COW - UNIT C

SUBCUTTING

Fabric		Strip Width	Pc #	Size
Background	☐	6-1/2"	13	5-1/2" x 1-1/2"
			16	4-1/2" x 5-1/2"
		4-1/2"	4	3-1/2" x 4-1/2"
			7	1-1/2" x 2-1/2"
			9	1-1/2" x 3-1/2"
			18	1-1/2" x 3-1/2"
			19	1-1/2" x 2-1/2"
		1-1/2"	1b	1-1/2" x 1-1/2"
			11	1-1/2" x 1-1/2"
			17a	1-1/2" x 1-1/2"
			20a	1-1/2" x 1-1/2"
Cow body & face	■	5-1/2"	14	7-1/2" x 3-1/2"
		1-1/2"	1a	1-1/2" x 1-1/2"
			3b	1-1/2" x 1-1/2"
Cow ear & far legs	■	2-1/2"	6	1-1/2" x 2-1/2"
			8	1-1/2" x 3-1/2"
			9a	1-1/2" x 1-1/2"
			10a	1-1/2" x 1-1/2"
			15a	1-1/2" x 1-1/2"
			17	2-1/2" x 3-1/2"
			18a	1-1/2" x 1-1/2"
			20	2-1/2" x 1-1/2"
			21a	1-1/2" x 1-1/2"
Udder	☐	4-1/2"	2a	1-1/2" x 1-1/2"
			3	5-1/2" x 4-1/2"
			4a	2-1/2" x 2-1/2"
			5	1-1/2" x 2-1/2"
			8a	1-1/2" x 1-1/2"
Cow belly, back, & near legs	☐	4-1/2"	2	1-1/2" x 4-1/2"
			3a	4-1/2" x 4-1/2"
		2-1/2"	1	2-1/2" x 8-1/2"
		1-1/2"	3c	1-1/2" x 1-1/2"
			4b	1-1/2" x 1-1/2"
			12a	1-1/2" x 1-1/2"
			14a,b	1-1/2" x 1-1/2"
			15	7-1/2" x 1-1/2"
Hooves	■	Scrap	10	2-1/2" x 1-1/2"
			12	2-1/2" x 1-1/2"
			21	2-1/2" x 1-1/2"

SEWING

1. 45 Flip - 1a, 1b, 2a, 3c, 4a, 4b, 8a, 9a, 10a, 12a, 14a, 14b, 15a, 17a, 18a, 20a, 21a.

2. Piggyback Flip - 3a, 3b.

3. 45 Joint - 5 to 6 to 7.

4. Sew 1 thru 21 together as shown to complete Unit C.

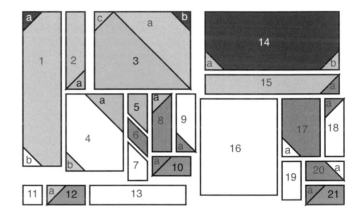

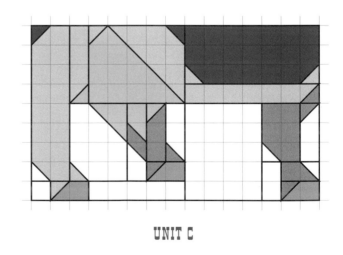

UNIT C

COW - UNIT D

SUBCUTTING

Fabric		Strip Width	Pc #	Size
Background	☐	4-1/2"	1a	2-1/2" x 2-1/2"
			4	4-1/2" x 4-1/2"
			19	2-1/2" x 3-1/2"
			23	4-1/2" x 8-1/2"
		1-1/2"	7	2-1/2" x 1-1/2"
			16a	1-1/2" x 1-1/2"
			17	1-1/2" x 3-1/2"
			18b	1-1/2" x 1-1/2"
			20	2-1/2" x 1-1/2"
			22	1-1/2" x 1-1/2"
Cow body & face	■	5-1/2"	3	4-1/2" x 2-1/2"
			8	6-1/2" x 5-1/2"
			13	5-1/2" x 2-1/2"
		2-1/2"	4a	2-1/2" x 2-1/2"
			10	3-1/2" x 2-1/2"
			11	2-1/2" x 1-1/2"
			15	1-1/2" x 2-1/2"
		1-1/2"	1b	1-1/2" x 1-1/2"
			5	1-1/2" x 1-1/2"
			9a,b	1-1/2" x 1-1/2"
			14a	1-1/2" x 1-1/2"
			18a	1-1/2" x 1-1/2"
Cow ear & far legs	■	2-1/2"	6	2-1/2" x 1-1/2"
			9	3-1/2" x 2-1/2"
Cow belly, back, & near legs	☐	4-1/2"	1	5-1/2" x 3-1/2"
			2	3-1/2" x 2-1/2"
			18	2-1/2" x 3-1/2"
		2-1/2"	13b	2-1/2" x 2-1/2"
			14	2-1/2" x 2-1/2"
			16	2-1/2" x 2-1/2"
			23a	2-1/2" x 2-1/2"
		1-1/2"	12	1-1/2" x 1-1/2"
			13a	1-1/2" x 1-1/2"
			17a	1-1/2" x 1-1/2"
			19a	1-1/2" x 1-1/2"
			21a	1-1/2" x 1-1/2"
			23b	1-1/2" x 1-1/2"
Hooves	■	Scrap	21	2-1/2" x 1-1/2"

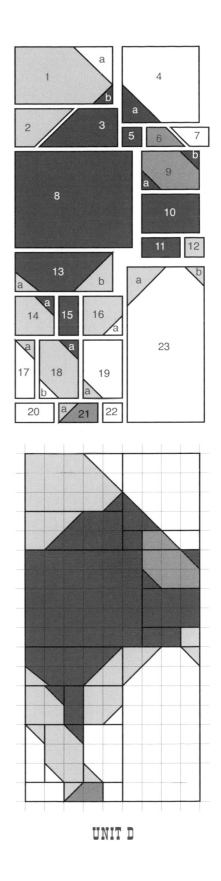

UNIT D

SEWING

1. 45 Flip - 1a, 1b, 4a, 9a, 9b, 13a, 13b, 14a, 16a, 17a, 18a, 18b, 19a, 21a, 23a, 23b.

2. 45 Joint - 2 to 3 and 6 to 7.

3. Sew 1 thru 23 together as shown to complete Unit D.

COW & CAT - UNIT E

SUBCUTTING

Fabric		Strip Width	Pc #	Size
Background	☐	6-1/2"	6	5-1/2" x 6-1/2"
			11	5-1/2" x 6-1/2"
		4-1/2"	1	8-1/2" x 4-1/2"
			2b	2-1/2" x 2-1/2"
			10	3-1/2" x 2-1/2"
			13	1-1/2" x 4-1/2"
		1-1/2"	2a	1-1/2" x 1-1/2"
			8	2-1/2" x 1-1/2"
			9a,b	1-1/2" x 1-1/2"
			12a	1-1/2" x 1-1/2"
			14a	1-1/2" x 1-1/2"
Cow body & face	■	5-1/2"	3	3-1/2" x 4-1/2"
		2-1/2"	5	2-1/2" x 1-1/2"
			6a	2-1/2" x 2-1/2"
			9	3-1/2" x 2-1/2"
		1-1/2"	7a	1-1/2" x 1-1/2"
Cow belly, back, & near legs	☐	4-1/2"	2	3-1/2" x 4-1/2"
		2-1/2"	7	2-1/2" x 1-1/2"
		1-1/2"	4	1-1/2" x 1-1/2"
Cat body	■	3-1/2"	12	3-1/2" x 2-1/2"
			14	2-1/2" x 4-1/2"
Cat far legs	☐	1-1/2"	10a	1-1/2" x 1-1/2"

SEWING

1. 45 Flip - 2a, 2b, 6a, 7a, 9a, 9b, 10a, 12a, 14a.
2. 45 Joint - 2 to 3.
3. Sew 1 thru 14 together as shown to complete Unit E.

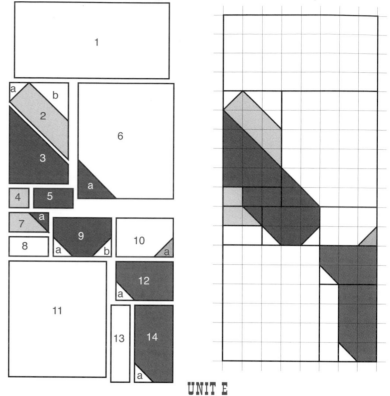

UNIT E

CAT LEG - UNIT F

SUBCUTTING

Fabric		Strip Width	Pc #	Size
Background	☐	4-1/2"	1	29-1/2" x 4-1/2"
			2a	2-1/2" x 2-1/2"
		1-1/2"	2b	1-1/2" x 1-1/2"
			3a,b	3/4" x 3/4"
			4	1-1/2" x 2-1/2"
			5a,b	3/4" X 3/4"
			6	1-1/2" x 1-1/2"
Cat body	■	3-1/2"	2	3-1/2" x 2-1/2"
			3	1-1/2" x 2-1/2"
Cat far legs	☐	1-1/2"	5	1-1/2" x 1-1/2"

SEWING

1. 45 Flip - 2a, 2b, 3a, 3b, 5a, 5b.

2. Sew 1 thru 6 together as shown to complete Unit F.

UNIT F

ASSEMBLY

Sew Unit B to Unit C and Unit D to Unit E. Sew B-C to D-E. Sew Unit A on top of B-E. Sew Unit F below A-E.

COW TAIL - BORDER 1

SUBCUTTING

Fabric		Strip Width	Pc #	Size
Border		8-1/2"	1	8-1/2" x 6-1/2"
			2	7-1/2" x 1-1/2"
			4	6-1/2" x 8-1/2"
			14	6-1/2" x 7-1/2"
			15	2-1/2" x 7-1/2"
		4-1/2"	16	5-1/2" x 4-1/2"
		2-1/2"	8	1-1/2" x 2-1/2"
			10	1-1/2" x 2-1/2"
			11	5-1/2" x 2-1/2"
			13	1-1/2" x 2-1/2"
			17	1-1/2" x 2-1/2"
			19	2-1/2" x 1-1/2"
			20	2-1/2" x 1-1/2"
			21	2-1/2" x 1-1/2"
		1-1/2"	6	1-1/2" x 3-1/2"
			22	3-1/2" x 1-1/2"
Cow body & face		2-1/2"	12	2-1/2" x 2-1/2"
		1-1/2"	3a	1-1/2" x 1-1/2"
			4a	1-1/2" x 1-1/2"
			9	1-1/2" x 7-1/2"
			8a	1-1/2" x 1-1/2"
			14a	1-1/2" x 1-1/2"
			15a	1-1/2" x 1-1/2"
Cow belly, back, & near legs		4-1/2"	5	1-1/2" x 3-1/2"
			7	1-1/2" x 3-1/2"
		2-1/2"	3	2-1/2" x 1-1/2"
Mouse		Scrap	18	1-1/2" x 2-1/2"
			19a	1" x 1"
			20a	1-1/2" x 1-1/2"
			21a	1" x 1"

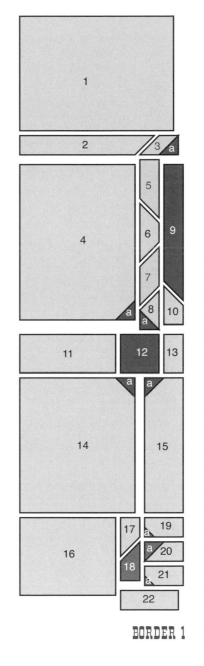

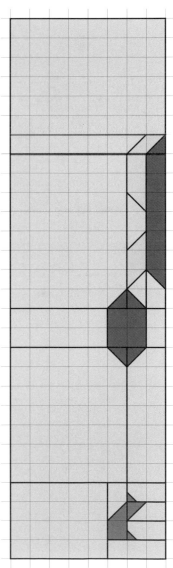

BORDER 1

SEWING

1. 45 Flip - 3a, 4a, 8a, 14a, 15a, 19a, 20a, 21a.

2. 45 Joint - 2 to 3, 5 to 6 to 7 to 8, 9 to 10, 17 to 18.

3. Sew 1 thru 22 together as shown to complete Border 1.

CAT - BORDER 2

SUBCUTTING

Fabric		Strip Width	Pc #	Size
Border	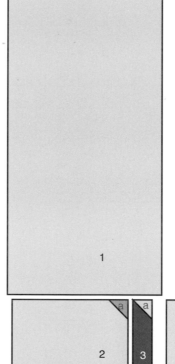	8-1/2"	1	8-1/2" x 16-1/2"
			2	6-1/2" x 5-1/2"
			3a	1-1/2" x 1-1/2"
			15a	1-1/2" x 1-1/2"
		4-1/2"	14	4-1/2" x 1-1/2"
		2-1/2"	7	3-1/2" x 2-1/2"
			9	1-1/2" x 2-1/2"
			10	2-1/2" x 1-1/2"
			12	2-1/2" x 1-1/2"
		1-1/2"	6	1-1/2" x 2-1/2"
			11a,b	3/4" x 3/4"
			15b,c	3/4" x 3/4"
			16	1-1/2" x 12-1/2"
Cat body		3-1/2"	3	1-1/2" x 5-1/2"
			4	7-1/2" x 3-1/2"
			5a	1-1/2" x 1-1/2"
			7a	1-1/2" x 1-1/2"
			8	2-1/2" x 2-1/2"
			9a,b	1-1/2" x 1-1/2"
			13	1-1/2" x 1-1/2"
			15	2-1/2" x 1-1/2"
Cat far legs		1-1/2"	2a	1-1/2" x 1-1/2"
			5	1-1/2" x 3-1/2"
			8a	1-1/2" x 1-1/2"
			11	2-1/2" x 1-1/2"

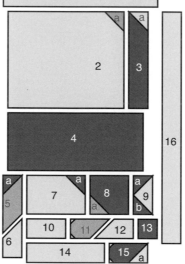

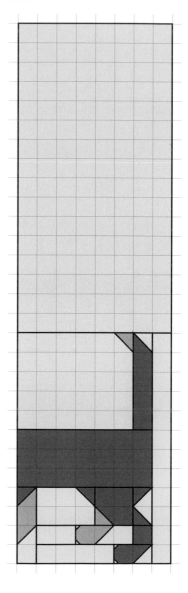

BORDER 2

SEWING

1. 45 Flip - 2a, 3a, 5a, 7a, 8a, 9a, 9b, 11a, 11b,15a, 15b, 15c.

2. 45 Joint - 5 to 6 and 11 to 12.
3. Sew 1 thru 16 as shown to compete Border 2.

BIRDS - BORDER 3

SUBCUTTING

Fabric		Strip Width	Pc #	Size
Border	☐	8-1/2"	1	4-1/2" x 8-1/2"
			3	(cut 2) 1-1/2" x 1-1/2"
			19	26-1/2" x 8-1/2"
		4-1/2"	2a	(cut 2) 3-1/2" x 3-1/2"
			14	4-1/2" x 4-1/2"
			17	3-1/2" x 4-1/2"
			18	9-1/2" x 4-1/2"
		2-1/2"	5	(cut 2) 3-1/2" x 2-1/2"
			9	(cut 2) 2-1/2" x 2-1/2"
			16	2-1/2" x 3-1/2"
		1-1/2"	7	(cut 2) 1-1/2" x 1-1/2"
			8a	(cut 2) 1-1/2" x 1-1/2"
			10	(cut 2) 2-1/2" x 1-1/2"
			13a	(cut 2) 1-1/2" x 1-1/2"
Bird body	▨	3-1/2"	2	(cut 2) 3-1/2" x 3-1/2"
			4	(cut 2) 1-1/2" x 2-1/2"
			6a	(cut 2) 1-1/2" x 1-1/2"
			11	(cut 2) 3-1/2" x 1-1/2"
			13	(cut 2) 4-1/2" x 1-1/2"
			14a	1-1/2" x 1-1/2"
			15	2-1/2" x 1-1/2"
			17a	1-1/2" x 1-1/2"
Bird wing	☐	2-1/2"	5a	(cut 2) 2-1/2" x 2-1/2"
			6	(cut 2) 2-1/2" x 1-1/2"
			8	(cut 2) 2-1/2" x 1-1/2"
			12	(cut 2) 3-1/2" x 1-1/2"

SEWING

1. 45 Flip - 5a, 6a, 8a, 13a, 14a, 17a.

2. Half Square - 2 and 2a.

3. 45 Joint - 10 to 11 to 12 to 13.

4. Sew 1 thru 17 together as shown.

5. For second bird repeat 2-13. Add 18 on top. (Pieces 14-17 on the second bird are included in Unit A.)

6. Sew the second bird to the first bird to complete Border 3.

BORDER 4
This border is a 48-1/2" x 4-1/2" strip of Border fabric. You may also piece this as you choose or leave it off.

ASSEMBLY
Sew Border 1 to the left of the cow. Sew Border 2 to the right of the cow. Sew Border 3 on top and Border 4 on bottom.

DETAILS
Embroider tail on mouse.

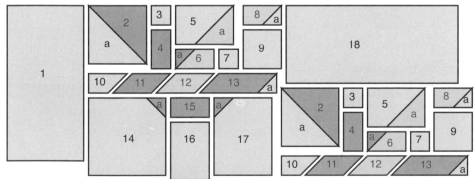

BORDER 3

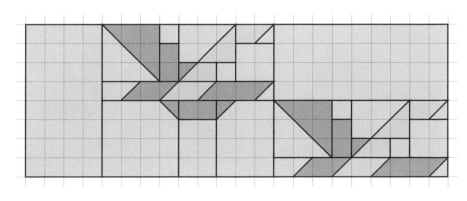

CUMBERLAND SUMMER
47" x 38"

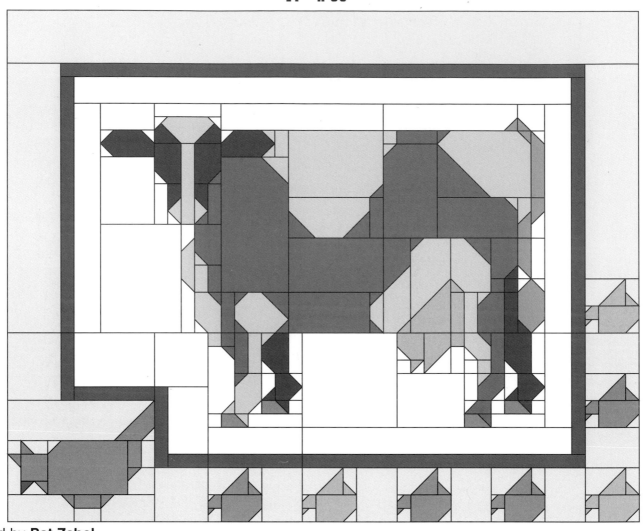

Designed by Pat Zabel
Steamboat Springs, Colorado

YARDAGE

3/4 yd.	☐	Background
1/8 yd.	■	Cow face, back legs
1/3 yd.	■	Cow body
1/3 yd.	▨	White spots
1/8 yd.	▨	Tail
1/8 yd.	▨	Udder
Scrap	▨	Hooves
1/4 yd.	▨	Hen
1/4 yd.	▨	Chicks
	☐	(or 2 different 1/8 yd.)
Scrap	■	Beak
1/4 yd.	■	Dark border
7/8 yd.	☐	Outer border
1/2 yd.		Binding
2-1/2 yds.		Backing

34

CUTTING

Cut all strips crosswise as shown in Rotary Cutting. Cut the following strips, then refer to each Unit's cutting chart for size of pieces to cut from each strip. Pieces may be subcut from a wider strip.

Fabric		# of Strips	Strip Width
Background	☐	1	7-1/2"
		4	2-1/2"
		3	1-1/2"
Cow face, back legs	■	1	2-1/2"
		1	1-1/2"

Cutting, cont.

Fabric		# of Strips	Strip Width
Cow body	■	1	5-1/2"
		1	3-1/2"
		1	1-1/2"
White spots	▨	1	5-1/2"
		1	2-1/2"
		1	1-1/2"
Tail	▨	1	2-1/2"
Udder	▨	1	3-1/2"
Dark Border	■	3	1-1/2"
Outer Border	☐	3	4-1/2"
		2	3-1/2"
		1	2-1/2"
		2	1-1/2"

CHICKEN AND CHICKS

1. Make seven chicks as explained on page 10, using 3-1/2" and 1-1/2" Outer border strips for the background.
2. Make a hen as directed on page 10, using 3-1/2", 2-1/2", and 1-1/2" Outer border strips for the background.
   Substitute the following pieces for the same # pieces on page 10: #11 - 5-1/2" x 2-1/2", #14 - 4-1/2" x 2-1/2";
   #16 - 2-1/2" x 1-1/2". Omit pieces 12, 13, 17, and the two chicks.

Note: The hen shown in Cumberland Summer is reversed from the hen on page 10.
   See page 7 in the general directions.

HEAD - UNIT A

SUBCUTTING

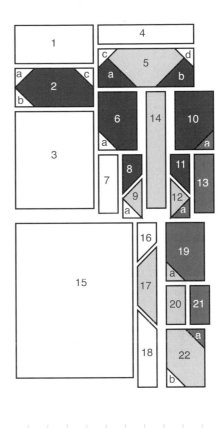

Fabric		Strip Width	Pc #	Size
Background	☐	7-1/2"	1	4-1/2" x 2-1/2"
			3	4-1/2" x 5-1/2"
			4	5-1/2" x 1-1/2"
			15	6-1/2" x 8-1/2"
			18	1-1/2" x 4-1/2"
		1-1/2"	2a,b,c	1-1/2" x 1-1/2"
			5c,d	1-1/2" x 1-1/2"
			6a	1-1/2" x 1-1/2"
			7	1-1/2" x 3-1/2"
			9a	1-1/2" x 1-1/2"
			16	1-1/2" x 2-1/2"
			22b	1-1/2" x 1-1/2"
Cow face, back legs	■	2-1/2"	2	4-1/2" x 2-1/2"
			5a,b	2-1/2" x 2-1/2"
			6	2-1/2" x 3-1/2"
			8	1-1/2" x 2-1/2"
			10	2-1/2" x 3-1/2"
			11	1-1/2" x 2-1/2"
Cow body	■	3-1/2"	13	1-1/2" x 3-1/2"
			19	2-1/2" x 3-1/2"
		1-1/2"	10a	1-1/2" x 1-1/2"
			12a	1-1/2" x 1-1/2"
			21	1-1/2" x 2-1/2"
			22a	1-1/2" x 1-1/2"
White spots	☐	5-1/2"	17	1-1/2" x 4-1/2"
		2-1/2"	5	5-1/2" x 2-1/2"
			9	1-1/2" x 2-1/2"
			12	1-1/2" x 2-1/2"
			20	1-1/2" x 2-1/2"
			22	2-1/2" x 3-1/2"
		1-1/2"	14	1-1/2" x 6-1/2"
			19a	1-1/2" x 1-1/2"

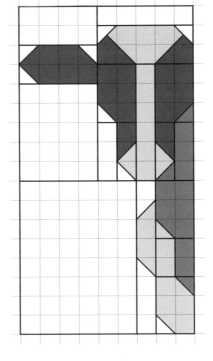

UNIT A

SEWING

1. 45 Flip - 2a, 2b, 2c, 6a, 9a, 10a, 12a, 19a, 22a, 22b.
2. Flips in Order - 5a, 5b, 5c, 5d.
3. 45 Joint - 8 to 9, 11 to 12, 16 to 17 to 18.
4. Sew 1 thru 22 together as shown to complete Unit A.

EAR & BACK – UNIT B

SUBCUTTING

Fabric		Strip Width	Pc #	Size
Background ☐		2-1/2"	12	12-1/2" x 2-1/2"
		1-1/2"	1a	1-1/2" x 1-1/2"
Cow face, back legs ■		2-1/2"	1	4-1/2" x 2-1/2"
Cow body ■		5-1/2"	3	5-1/2" x 10-1/2"
			9	7-1/2" x 4-1/2"
		3-1/2"	4	1-1/2" x 3-1/2"
			5b	2-1/2" x 2-1/2"
			7a,b	2-1/2" x 2-1/2"
			8	1-1/2" x 3-1/2"
			10	6-1/2" x 3-1/2"
		1-1/2"	5a,c,d	1-1/2" x 1-1/2"
			6a	1-1/2" x 1-1/2"
			11a,b	1-1/2" x 1-1/2"
White spots ☐		5-1/2"	5	4-1/2" x 3-1/2"
			6	7-1/2" x 5-1/2"
			7	6-1/2" x 3-1/2"
		2-1/2"	2	1-1/2" x 2-1/2"
			3a	2-1/2" x 2-1/2"
		1-1/2"	1b,c	1-1/2" x 1-1/2"
			11	1-1/2" x 3-1/2"

SEWING

1. 45 Flip - 1a, 1b, 1c, 3a, 5a, 5b, 5c, 5d, 6a, 7a, 7b, 11a, 11b.

12. Sew 1 thru 12 together as shown to complete Unit B.

RUMP – UNIT C

SUBCUTTING

Fabric		Strip Width	Pc #	Size
Background ☐		2-1/2"	11	10-1/2" x 2-1/2"
			12	2-1/2" x 2-1/2"
		1-1/2"	5a	1-1/2" x 1-1/2"
			10	1-1/2" x 2-1/2"
Cow body ■		5-1/2"	3	4-1/2" x 7-1/2"
			4c	4-1/2" x 4-1/2"
		3-1/2"	2	3-1/2" x 1-1/2"
			6	6-1/2" x 3-1/2"
		1-1/2"	4a	1-1/2" x 1-1/2"

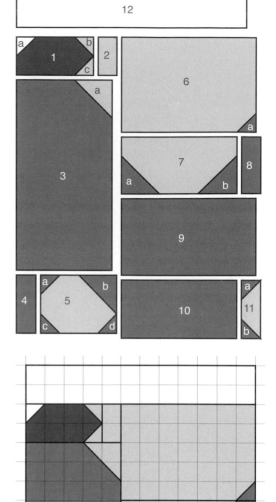

UNIT B

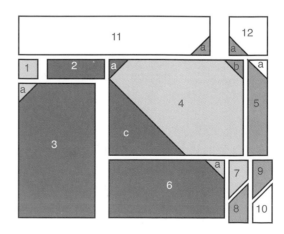

UNIT C

UNIT C CONT.

SUBCUTTING

Fabric		Strip Width	Pc #	Size
White spots	▨	5-1/2"	4	7-1/2" x 5-1/2"
		2-1/2"	7	1-1/2" x 2-1/2"
		1-1/2"	1	1-1/2" x 1-1/2"
			3a	1-1/2" x 1-1/2"
			6a	1-1/2" x 1-1/2"
Tail	▨	2-1/2"	4b	1-1/2" x 1-1/2"
			5	1-1/2" x 5-1/2"
			8	1-1/2" x 2-1/2"
			9	1-1/2" x 2-1/2"
			11a	1-1/2" x 1-1/2"
			12a	1-1/2" x 1-1/2"

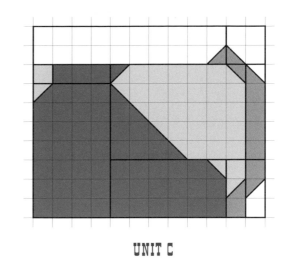

UNIT C

SEWING

1. 45 Flip - 3a, 4a, 4b, 4c, 5a, 6a, 11a, 12a.
2. 45 Joint - 7 to 8, 9 to 10.
3. Sew 1 thru 12 together as shown to complete Unit C.

TAIL - UNIT D

SUBCUTTING

Fabric		Strip Width	Pc #	Size
Background	☐	1-1/2"	13a	1-1/2" x 1-1/2"
			14	1-1/2" x 3-1/2"
			15a,b,d	1-1/2" x 1-1/2"
Cow face, back legs	■	1-1/2"	6a	1-1/2" x 1-1/2"
			8	1-1/2" x 1-1/2"
			12	1-1/2" x 3-1/2"
			15c	1-1/2" x 1-1/2"
Cow body	▨	5-1/2"	1	2-1/2" x 4-1/2"
			11	2-1/2" x 3-1/2"
		3-1/2"	5a	2-1/2" x 2-1/2"
			6	2-1/2" x 3-1/2"
		1-1/2"	3a	1-1/2" x 1-1/2"
			7	1-1/2" x 1-1/2"
White spots	▨	5-1/2"	2	2-1/2" x 5-1/2"
			3	3-1/2" x 6-1/2"
			5	3-1/2" x 4-1/2"
		1-1/2"	10	1-1/2" x 3-1/2"
			11a	1-1/2" x 1-1/2"
Tail	▨	2-1/2"	13	1-1/2" x 3-1/2"
			15	2-1/2" x 4-1/2"
Udder	▨	3-1/2"	2a	1-1/2" x 1-1/2"
			4	3-1/2" x 4-1/2"
			5b	1-1/2" x 1-1/2"
			9	1-1/2" x 3-1/2"

SEWING

1. 45 Flip - 2a, 3a, 5a, 5b, 6a, 11a, 13a, 15a, 15b, 15c, 15d.
2. 45 Joint - 1 to 2, 3 to 4.
3. Sew 1 thru 15 together as shown to complete Unit D.

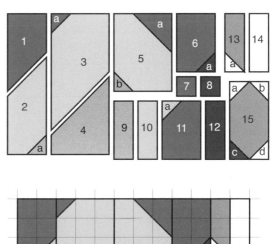

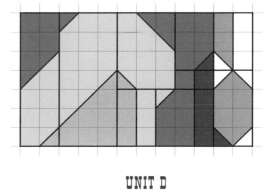

UNIT D

FRONT LEGS - UNIT E

SUBCUTTING

Fabric		Strip Width	Pc #	Size
Background	☐	7-1/2"	3	6-1/2" x 4-1/2"
			6	4-1/2" x 4-1/2"
			7	3-1/2" x 5-1/2"
		2-1/2"	13	2-1/2" x 5-1/2"
			26	7-1/2" x 2-1/2"
		1-1/2"	16b	1-1/2" x 1-1/2"
			17b	1-1/2" x 1-1/2"
			18	1-1/2" x 3-1/2"
			19	1-1/2" x 2-1/2"
			20a,b	1-1/2" x 1-1/2"
			22	1-1/2" x 1-1/2"
			23	1-1/2" x 1-1/2"
			25	4-1/2" x 1-1/2"
Cow face, back legs	■	2-1/2"	17	2-1/2" x 3-1/2"
			20	2-1/2" x 2-1/2"
		1-1/2"	19a	1-1/2" x 1-1/2"
			21a	1-1/2" x 1-1/2"
Cow body	■	3-1/2"	14	1-1/2" x 3-1/2"
		1-1/2"	12	1-1/2" x 1-1/2"
			13a	1-1/2" x 1-1/2"
			16a	1-1/2" x 1-1/2"
White spots	☐	2-1/2"	16	2-1/2" x 3-1/2"
		1-1/2"	11	1-1/2" x 1-1/2"
			13b	1-1/2" x 1-1/2"
			15	1-1/2" x 3-1/2"
			17a	1-1/2" x 1-1/2"
			24a	1-1/2" x 1-1/2"
Hooves	■	Scraps	21	2-1/2" x 1-1/2"
			24	2-1/2" x 1-1/2"
Dark border	■	1-1/2"	2	1-1/2" x 5-1/2"
			4	6-1/2" x 1-1/2"
			8	3-1/2" x 1-1/2"
			9	1-1/2" x 6-1/2"
			27	7-1/2" x 1-1/2"
Outer border	☐	4-1/2"	1	4-1/2" x 5-1/2"
			10	4-1/2" x 4-1/2"
			29	3-1/2" x 4-1/2"
Chick	■		28	See page 35
Chicken	■		5	See page 35

SEWING

1. 45 Flip - 13a, 13b, 16a, 16b, 17a, 17b, 19a, 20a, 20b, 21a, 24a.
2. Sew 1 thru 29 together as shown to complete Unit E.

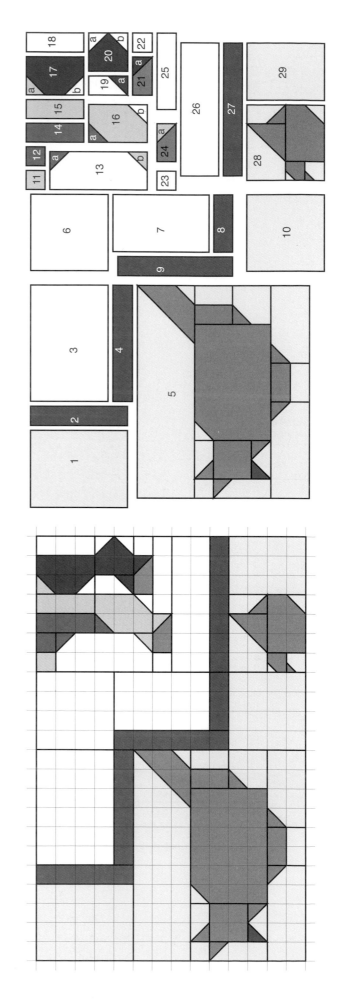

REAR LEGS - UNIT F

SUBCUTTING

Fabric		Strip Width	Pc #	Size
Background	☐	7-1/2"	1	7-1/2" x 7-1/2"
			14	5-1/2" x 4-1/2"
		2-1/2"	5a	2-1/2" x 2-1/2"
			25	2-1/2" x 7-1/2"
			26	20-1/2" x 2-1/2"
		1-1/2"	2a	1-1/2" x 1-1/2"
			3	1-1/2" x 1-1/2"
			4a	1-1/2" x 1-1/2"
			7	1-1/2" x 2-1/2"
			8b	1-1/2" x 1-1/2"
			9	1-1/2" x 1-1/2"
			12a	1-1/2" x 1-1/2"
			13	1-1/2" x 3-1/2"
			15	1-1/2" x 2-1/2"
			16b	1-1/2" x 1-1/2"
			17	1-1/2" x 2-1/2"
			18a,b	1-1/2" x 1-1/2"
			19a	1-1/2" x 1-1/2"
			20	1-1/2" x 1-1/2"
			22	1-1/2" x 1-1/2"
			24	4-1/2" x 1-1/2"
Cow face, back legs	■	2-1/2"	12	2-1/2" x 3-1/2"
			18	2-1/2" x 2-1/2"
		1-1/2"	17a	1-1/2" x 1-1/2"
			21a	1-1/2" x 1-1/2"
Cow body	■	3-1/2"	11	1-1/2" x 3-1/2"
			16	2-1/2" x 2-1/2"
		1-1/2"	8a	1-1/2" x 1-1/2"
			19	2-1/2" x 1-1/2"
			23a	1-1/2" x 1-1/2"
White spots	☐	2-1/2"	8	2-1/2" x 2-1/2"
		1-1/2"	10	1-1/2" x 1-1/2"
			16a	1-1/2" x 1-1/2"
Udder	☐	3-1/2"	2	2-1/2" x 2-1/2"
			4	1-1/2" x 1-1/2"
			5	2-1/2" x 3-1/2"
			6	1-1/2" x 1-1/2"
Hooves	■	Scraps	21	2-1/2" x 1-1/2"
			23	2-1/2" x 1-1/2"
Dark Border	■	1-1/2"	27	1-1/2" x 9-1/2"
			28	21-1/2" x 1-1/2"
Outer Border	☐	4-1/2"	30, 32,	3-1/2" x 4-1/2"
			34	3-1/2" x 4-1/2"
Chick			29, 31, 33 - see page 35

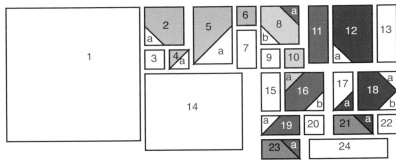

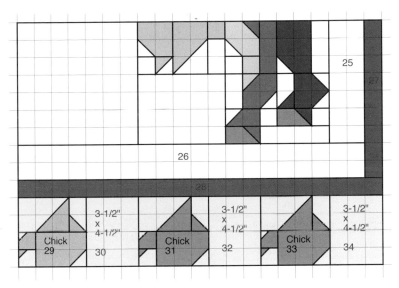

UNIT F

Mid-afternoon watering tank, pumped by the windmill.

SEWING

1. 45 flip - 2a, 4a, 5a, 8a, 8b, 12a, 16a, 16b, 17a, 18a, 18b, 19a, 21a, 23a.
2. Sew 1 thru 34 together as shown to complete Unit F.

ASSEMBLY

SUBCUTTING

Fabric	Strip Width	# to Cut	Size
Outer Border	4-1/2"	2	4-1/2" x 3-1/2"
		1	4-1/2" x 16-1/2"
		1	4-1/2" x 20-1/2"
		1	47-1/2" x 4-1/2"

1. Sew Unit A to Unit B and Unit C to Unit D. Sew Units A-B to C-D.

2. Sew a 2-1/2" background border to both sides and to the top of A-D.

3. Sew a 1-1/2" Dark border along these same three sides.

4. Sew a 20-1/2" x 4-1/2" Outer border to the left side.

5. Sew Unit E to Unit F. Attach this below the unit in Step 4.

6. Sew two 4-1/2" x 3-1/2" Outer border pieces together with three chicks. Add a plain Outer border piece which measures 4-1/2" x 16-1/2" on top of the chicks and attach to the right edge of the quilt.

7. Attach a 47-1/2" x 4-1/2" Outer border to the top.

DETAILS

Make eyes on the chicks with french knots.

Ayliffe and Eva trailing Coke's cattle from the high country to home.

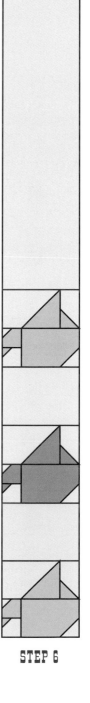

STEP 6

40

BUTTERCUP AND BABY
36" x 32"

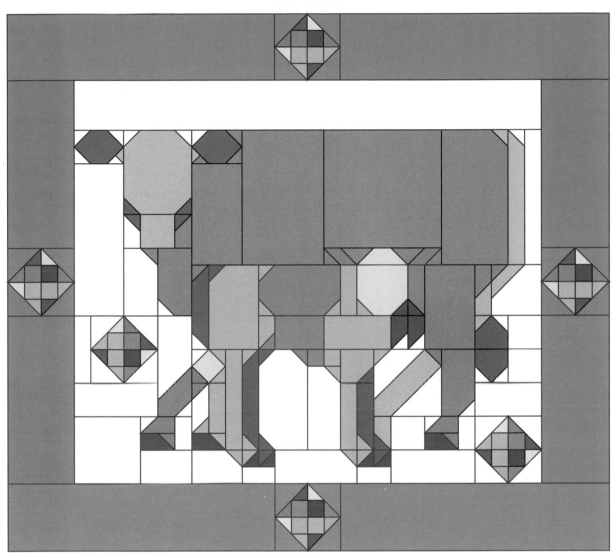

YARDAGE

1/2 yd.	☐	Background
1/4 yd.	▨	Heifer face & far legs
3/8 yd.	▨	Heifer body
1/8 yd.	▨	Heifer ears & tail
Scrap	▨	Udder
Scraps	▨	Hooves
1/8 yd.	▨	Calf face
1/8 yd.	▨	Calf rump & legs
1/8 yd.	▨	Calf belly
1/8 yd.	▨	Calf far legs & tail
1/2 yd.	▨	Border
1/3 yd.		Binding
1-1/8 yds.		Backing

Assorted 1-1/2" Scraps for Sweet Sixteen Blocks

CUTTING

Cut all strips crosswise as shown in Rotary Cutting. Cut the following strips, then refer to each Unit's cutting chart for size of pieces to cut from each strip. Pieces may be subcut from a wider strip.

Fabric		# of Strips	Strip Width
Background	☐	1	4-1/2"
		2	2-1/2"
		1	1-1/2"
Heifer face & far legs	▨	1	4-1/2"
Heifer body	▨	1	7-1/2"
		1	1-1/2"

Cutting, cont.

Fabric		# of Strips	Strip Width
Heifer ears & tail	▨	1	2-1/2"
Calf face	▨	1	3-1/2"
Calf rump & legs	▨	1	3-1/2"
Calf belly	▨	1	3-1/2"
Calf far legs & tail	▨	1	1-1/2"

Sweet Sixteen Blocks
Assorted 1-1/2" Scraps

Border	▨	3	4-1/2"
		1	2-1/2"

SWEET SIXTEEN BLOCKS

If you want to use the 4" Sweet Sixteen blocks, make them now. Make two with background corners and four with border corners. If you prefer, substitute 4-1/2" squares of background or border for these blocks.

1. Cut 1-1/2" squares of scraps and sew together in sets of two. Each block uses sixteen 1-1/2" squares.
2. Mix up the sets and sew into six 16-patch blocks.
3. Cut eight 2-1/2" background squares and sixteen 2-1/2" border squares. Use these as 45 Flips on the 16-patch blocks.

HEIFER HEAD - UNIT A

SUBCUTTING

Fabric	Strip Width	Pc #	Size
Background ☐	4-1/2"	2	3-1/2" x 9-1/2"
		7	2-1/2" x 4-1/2"
		9	1-1/2" x 4-1/2"
		14	4-1/2" x 4-1/2"
		18	3-1/2" x 2-1/2"
	2-1/2"	4	1-1/2" x 2-1/2"
		11	5-1/2" x 2-1/2"
		12	2-1/2" x 5-1/2"
		17	1-1/2" x 2-1/2"
	1-1/2"	1a,b,c,d	1-1/2" x 1-1/2"
		3a,b	1-1/2" x 1-1/2"
		8a	1-1/2" x 1-1/2"
		13a	1-1/2" x 1-1/2"
		15a	1-1/2" x 1-1/2"
		10	Sweet Sixteen Block
Heifer face & far legs	4-1/2"	1e	1-1/2" x 1-1/2"
		3	4-1/2" x 5-1/2"
		5	2-1/2" x 2-1/2"
Heifer body ▨	7-1/2"	8	2-1/2" x 4-1/2"
		13	2-1/2" x 3-1/2"
	1-1/2"	6	1-1/2" x 2-1/2"
		7a	1-1/2" x 1-1/2"
		15	2-1/2" x 1-1/2"
		16a	1-1/2" x 1-1/2"
Heifer ears & tail ■	2-1/2"	1	3-1/2" x 2-1/2"
		3c,d	1-1/2" x 1-1/2"
		4a	1-1/2" x 1-1/2"
		6a	1-1/2" x 1-1/2"
Hoof ■	Scrap	16	2-1/2" x 1-1/2"

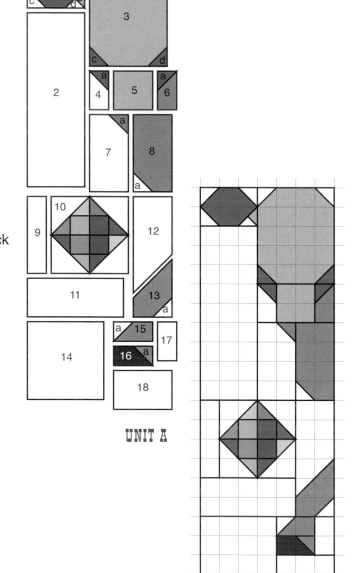

UNIT A

SEWING

1. 45 Flip - 1a, 1b, 1c, 3a, 3b, 3c, 3d, 4a, 6a, 7a, 8a, 13a, 15a, 16a.
2. 45 Joint - 12 to 13.
3. Half Square Flip - Make a Half Square with 1d and 1e; 45 Flip it to 1.
4. Sew 1 thru 18 together as shown to complete Unit A. Use either a Sweet Sixteen block for 10 or a 4-1/2" background square.

HEIFER BODY - UNIT B

SUBCUTTING

Fabric		Strip Width	Pc #	Size
Background	☐	1-1/2"	1a	1-1/2" x 1-1/2"
			11a	1-1/2" x 1-1/2"
			12	1-1/2" x 8-1/2"
Heifer face & far legs	◻	1-1/2"	1c	1-1/2" x 1-1/2"
			10a	1-1/2" x 1-1/2"
			11	1-1/2" x 8-1/2"
Heifer body	◼	7-1/2"	2	3-1/2" x 6-1/2"
			3	5-1/2" x 8-1/2"
			4	7-1/2" x 7-1/2"
			10	4-1/2" x 8-1/2"
		1-1/2"	1b,d,e	1-1/2" x 1-1/2"
			5a	1-1/2" x 1-1/2"
			6	2-1/2" x 1-1/2"
			8	2-1/2" x 1-1/2"
			9a	1-1/2" x 1-1/2"
Heifer ears & tail	◼	2-1/2"	1	3-1/2" x 2-1/2"
Calf face	◻	3-1/2"	7	3-1/2" x 1-1/2"
Calf belly	◼	3-1/2"	5	2-1/2" x 1-1/2"
			9	2-1/2" x 1-1/2"

SEWING

1. 45 Flip - 1a, 1b, 1e, 5a, 9a, 10a, 11a.

2. 45 Joint - 5 to 6 to 7 to 8 to 9.

3. Half Square Flip - Make a Half Square with 1c and 1d; 45 Flip it to 1.

4. Sew 1 thru 12 together as shown to complete Unit B.

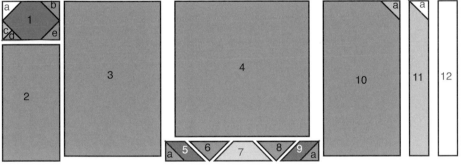

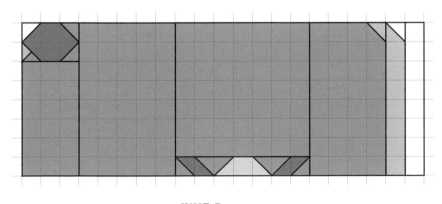

UNIT B

Cousin Lowell Wheeler Whiteman showing off Brown Swiss heifer and her pretty new baby, circa 1928.

CALF - UNIT C

SUBCUTTING

Fabric		Strip Width	Pc #	Size
Background	☐	4-1/2"	15	3-1/2" x 3-1/2"
		2-1/2"	17	2-1/2" x 2-1/2"
		1-1/2"	1b	1-1/2" x 1-1/2"
			10a	1-1/2" x 1-1/2"
			11a	1-1/2" x 1-1/2"
			16b	1-1/2" x 1-1/2"
Heifer face & far legs	◨	4-1/2"	14	1-1/2" x 2-1/2"
			15a	2-1/2" x 2-1/2"
			16a	1-1/2" x 1-1/2"
Heifer body	◩	7-1/2"	12	3-1/2" x 5-1/2"
		1-1/2"	1a	1-1/2" x 1-1/2"
			6	1-1/2" x 3-1/2"
			13	1-1/2" x 2-1/2"
			15b	1-1/2" x 1-1/2"
Heifer ears & tail	◼	2-1/2"	16	2-1/2" x 2-1/2"
Udder	◼	Scraps	5b	1-1/2" x 1-1/2"
			6a	1-1/2" x 1-1/2"
			10	1-1/2" x 2-1/2"
			11	1-1/2" x 2-1/2"
Calf face	◻	3-1/2"	5	3-1/2" x 3-1/2"
Calf rump & legs	◨	3-1/2"	2	3-1/2" x 5-1/2"
			3a,b,c	1-1/2" x 1-1/2"
			4	1-1/2" x 3-1/2"
			5a	1-1/2" x 1-1/2"
			7	1-1/2" x 2-1/2"
			9	4-1/2" x 2-1/2"
Calf belly	◨	3-1/2"	3	5-1/2" x 3-1/2"
			7a	1-1/2" x 1-1/2"
			8	3-1/2" x 2-1/2"
Calf far legs & tail	◼	1-1/2"	1	1-1/2" x 5-1/2"
			2a	1-1/2" x 1-1/2"

SEWING
(see illustrations on next page)
1. 45 Flip - 1a, 1b, 2a, 3a, 3b, 3c, 5a, 5b, 6a, 7a, 10a, 11a, 16a, 16b.
2. Piggyback flip - 15a, 15b.
3. 45 Joint - 13 to 14.
4. Sew 1 thru 17 together as shown to complete Unit C.

44

LEGS - UNIT D

SUBCUTTING

Fabric		Strip Width	Pc #	Size
Background	☐	4-1/2"	7	3-1/2" x 6-1/2"
			14a,c	3-1/2" x 3-1/2"
			32	4-1/2" x 2-1/2"
		2-1/2"	10	2-1/2" x 5-1/2"
			17	2-1/2" x 2-1/2"
			20	1-1/2" x 2-1/2"
			21	3-1/2" x 2-1/2"
			24	2-1/2" x 1-1/2"
			25	5-1/2" x 2-1/2"
			28	2-1/2" x 1-1/2"
			29	5-1/2" x 2-1/2"
			31	2-1/2" x 2-1/2"
		1-1/2"	1a	1-1/2" x 1-1/2"
			2	1-1/2" x 3-1/2"
			15a	1-1/2" x 1-1/2"
			18a	1-1/2" x 1-1/2"
			30a,b	1-1/2" x 1-1/2"
			33	Sweet 16 Block
Heifer face & far legs	◨	4-1/2"	1d	1-1/2" x 1-1/2"
			2b	1-1/2" x 1-1/2"
			3	1-1/2" x 3-1/2"
			4a	1-1/2" x 1-1/2"
			14	4-1/2" x 4-1/2"
			16	1-1/2" x 2-1/2"
Heifer body	◩	7-1/2"	15	2-1/2" x 4-1/2"
		1-1/2"	1c	1-1/2" x 1-1/2"
			2a	1-1/2" x 1-1/2"
			14d	1-1/2" x 1-1/2"
			18	2-1/2" x 1-1/2"
			19a	1-1/2" x 1-1/2"
Heifer ears & tail	◼	2-1/2"	30	2-1/2" x 2-1/2"
Hooves	◼	Scraps	4	2-1/2" x 1-1/2"
			19	2-1/2" x 1-1/2"
Calf face	◻	3-1/2"	1	2-1/2" x 2-1/2"
Calf belly	◨	3-1/2"	7b	1-1/2" x 1-1/2"
			8	1-1/2" x 1-1/2"
Calf far legs & tail	◼	1-1/2"	6	1-1/2" x 6-1/2"
			7a,c	1-1/2" x 1-1/2"
			11a	1-1/2" x 1-1/2"
			13	1-1/2" x 4-1/2"
			16a	1-1/2" x 1-1/2"
			23	1-1/2" x 1-1/2"
			27	1-1/2" x 1-1/2"

Subcutting, cont.

Fabric		Strip Width	Pc #	Size
Calf rump & legs	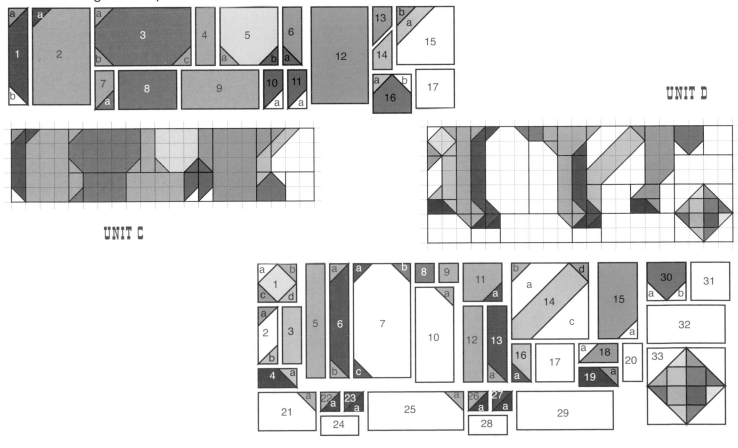	3-1/2"	1b	1-1/2" x 1-1/2"
			5	1-1/2" x 6-1/2"
			6a,b	1-1/2" x 1-1/2"
			9	1-1/2" x 1-1/2"
			10a	1-1/2" x 1-1/2"
			11	2-1/2" x 2-1/2"
			12	1-1/2" x 4-1/2"
			13a	1-1/2" x 1-1/2"
			14b	1-1/2" x 1-1/2"
			21a	1-1/2" x 1-1/2"
			22	1-1/2" x 1-1/2"
			25a	1-1/2" x 1-1/2"
			26	1-1/2" x 1-1/2"
Calf Hoof		Scrap	22a	1-1/2" x 1-1/2"
			23a	1-1/2" x 1-1/2"
			26a	1-1/2" x 1-1/2"
			27a	1-1/2" x 1-1/2"

SEWING

1. 45 Flip - 1a, 1b, 1c, 1d, 2a, 2b, 4a, 6a, 6b, 7a, 7b, 7c, 10a, 11a, 13a, 15a, 16a, 18a, 19a, 21a, 25a, 30a, 30b.
2. Half Squares - 22a,22b; 23a,23b; 26a,26b; 27a,27b.
3. Piggyback Flip - 14a, 14b.
4. Flips in Order - 14c, 14d.
5. Sew 1 thru 33 together as shown to complete Unit D. Use either a Sweet Sixteen block for 33 or a 4-1/2" background square.

ASSEMBLY

Assemble Units B, C, and D. Add Unit A to left of B-D. Sew a 28-1/2" x 3-1/2" background strip to the top. Add borders like ours or one of your own.

BORDER

Subcutting

Fabric		Strip Width	#of pcs.	Size
Border		4-1/2"	4	4-1/2" x 10-1/2"
			4	16-1/2" x 4-1/2"

SEWING

1. For each side border sew a 4-1/2" x 10-1/2" border to opposite sides of a Sweet Sixteen Block. Sew these to the sides of the quilt.
2. Sew the 16-1/2" x 4-1/2" border pieces to opposite sides of Sweet Sixteen Blocks. Sew these to the top and bottom of the quilt.

DETAILS

Embroider brands on your heifer and calf if you wish.

UNIT C

UNIT D

45

FRED AND SONNY
55" x 45"

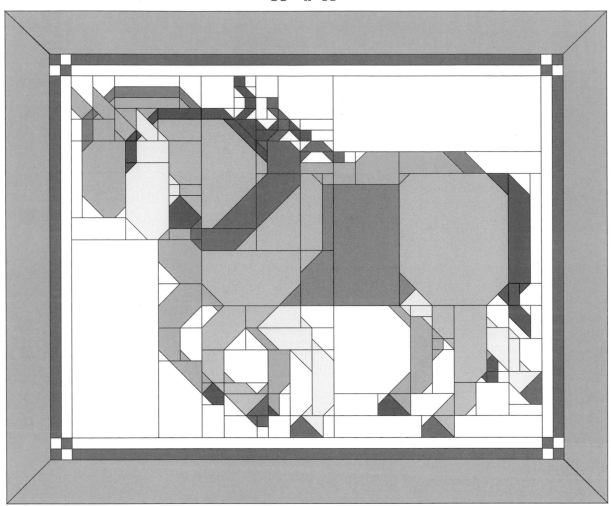

YARDAGE

1-1/4 yds.	☐	Background
1/3 yd.	▨	Far horse body
1/8 yd.	▨	Far horse mane & tail
1/8 yd.	▨	Far horse collar & hooves
1/2 yd.	▨	Near horse neck & rump
1/8 yd.	▨	Near horse mane & tail
1/4 yd.	▨	Near horse belly
1/4 yd.	☐	Near horse face & legs
1/4 yd.	▨	Near horse collar & hooves
1/4 yd.	▨	Inner border
3/4 yd.	▨	Outer border
1/2 yd.		Binding
2-7/8 yds.		Backing

CUTTING

Cut all strips crosswise as shown in Rotary Cutting. Cut the following strips, then refer to each Unit's cutting chart for size of pieces to cut from each strip. Pieces may be subcut from a wider strip.

Fabric		# of Strips	Strip Width
Background	☐	1	8-1/2"
		1	7-1/2"
		3	2-1/2"
		3	1-1/2"
Far horse body	▨	1	4-1/2"
		1	2-1/2"
		1	1-1/2"
Far horse mane & tail	▨	1	2-1/2"

Cutting, cont.

Fabric		# of Strips	Strip Width
Far horse collar & hooves	▨	1	3-1/2"
Near horse neck & rump	▨	1	10-1/2"
		1	2-1/2"
		1	1-1/2"
Near horse mane & tail	▨	1	3-1/2"
Near horse belly	▨	1	6-1/2"
Near horse face & legs	☐	1	5-1/2"
		1	1-1/2"
Near horse collar & hooves	▨	1	4-1/2"
		1	1-1/2"

46

HORSE HEADS - UNIT A
SUBCUTTING

Fabric		Strip Width	Pc #	Size
Background	☐	2-1/2"	1	2-1/2" x 3-1/2"
			3	2-1/2" x 3-1/2"
			11	2-1/2" x 3-1/2"
			17b	2-1/2" x 2-1/2"
			18	5-1/2" x 2-1/2"
			21b	2-1/2" x 2-1/2"
		1-1/2"	2a	1-1/2" x 1-1/2"
			5	1-1/2" x 2-1/2"
			8	6-1/2" x 1-1/2"
			16	1-1/2" x 7-1/2"
			17c	1-1/2" x 1-1/2"
Far horse body	▨	4-1/2"	2	2-1/2" x 3-1/2"
			4	2-1/2" x 3-1/2"
			17	4-1/2" x 7-1/2"
		2-1/2"	7	2-1/2" x 2-1/2"
			12a	2-1/2" x 2-1/2"
			13a	2-1/2" x 2-1/2"
			26	2-1/2" x 1-1/2"
		1-1/2"	3b	1-1/2" x 1-1/2"
			4b	1-1/2" x 1-1/2"
			10	6-1/2" x 1-1/2"
			11b	1-1/2" x 1-1/2"
			12b	1-1/2" x 1-1/2"
			21c	1-1/2" x 1-1/2"
Far horse mane & tail	▨	2-1/2"	2b	1-1/2" x 1-1/2"
			3a	2-1/2" x 2-1/2"
			4a	1-1/2" x 1-1/2"
			6	1-1/2" x 2-1/2"
			9	6-1/2" x 1-1/2"
			11a	2-1/2" x 2-1/2"
			17a	1-1/2" x 1-1/2"
Far horse collar & hooves	■	3-1/2"	25	3-1/2" x 3-1/2"
Near horse neck & rump	☐	10-1/2"	22	3-1/2" x 4-1/2"
		2-1/2"	12	2-1/2" x 3-1/2"
			15	4-1/2" x 2-1/2"
			25b	2-1/2" x 2-1/2"
		1-1/2"	13c	1-1/2" x 1-1/2"
			24	2-1/2" x 1-1/2"
Near horse mane & tail	■	3-1/2"	12c	1-1/2" x 1-1/2"
			13b	2-1/2" x 2-1/2"
			13d	1-1/2" x 1-1/2"
			14	4-1/2" x 1-1/2"
			19	1-1/2" x 2-1/2"
			21a	1-1/2" x 1-1/2"
Near horse collar & hooves	■	1-1/2"	25c	1-1/2" x 1-1/2"
			27	1-1/2" x 1-1/2"

Subcutting, cont.

Fabric		Strip Width	Pc #	Size
Near horse face & legs	☐	5-1/2"	13	2-1/2" x 3-1/2"
			20	3-1/2" x 2-1/2"
			21	4-1/2" x 7-1/2"
		1-1/2"	13e	1-1/2" x 1-1/2"
			15a	1-1/2" x 1-1/2"
			22a	1-1/2" x 1-1/2"
			23	1-1/2" x 1-1/2"
			25a	1-1/2" x 1-1/2"

SEWING

1. 45 Flip - 2a, 2b, 12a, 12b, 12c, 15a, 17a, 17b, 17c, 21a, 21b, 21c, 22a, 25a, 25b, 25c.
2. Piggyback Flip - 3a, 3b; 11a, 11b.
3. 45 Joint - 1 to 2, 3 to 4.
4. Half Square Flip - Make a Half Square with 4a and 4b, use this as a Half Square Flip on 4. Make a Half Square of 13a and 13b. Add 13c flip to 13b, then use this set as an upper right flip for 13. Make a Half Square of 13d and 13e, and use it as a lower left flip for 13.
5. Sew 1 thru 27 together as shown to complete Unit A.

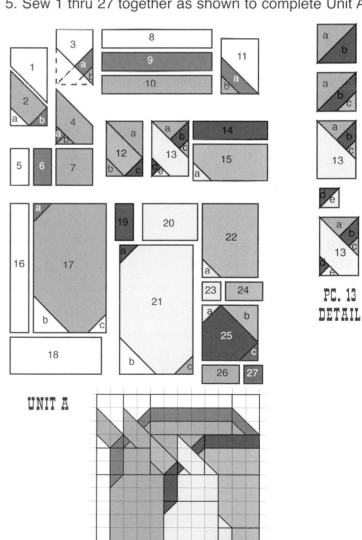

PC. 13 DETAIL

UNIT A

COLLARS - UNIT B

SUBCUTTING

Fabric		Strip Width	Pc #	Size
Background	☐	7-1/2"	1	3-1/2" x 3-1/2"
			10	1-1/2" x 2-1/2"
			13	5-1/2" x 4-1/2"
		2-1/2"	9	2-1/2" x 2-1/2"
		1-1/2"	2a	1-1/2" x 1-1/2"
			4	1-1/2" x 1-1/2"
			5a,b	1-1/2" x 1-1/2"
			6	1-1/2" x 1-1/2"
			8a,b	1-1/2" x 1-1/2"
			12a	1-1/2" x 1-1/2"
			16	2-1/2" x 1-1/2"
			18a	1-1/2" x 1-1/2"
			21	2-1/2" x 1-1/2"
			24a	1-1/2" x 1-1/2"
			25	3-1/2" x 1-1/2"
			27	2-1/2" x 1-1/2"
			28a,b	1-1/2" x 1-1/2"
			29	3-1/2" x 1-1/2"
Far horse body	▧	4-1/2"	30	3-1/2" x 1-1/2"
		1-1/2"	33a	1-1/2" x 1-1/2"
			34	1-1/2" x 1-1/2"
Far horse collar & hooves	▨	3-1/2"	3	1-1/2" x 1-1/2"
			5	2-1/2" x 1-1/2"
			7	1-1/2" x 1-1/2"
			8	2-1/2" x 1-1/2"
			14b	2-1/2" x 2-1/2"
			16a,b	1-1/2" x 1-1/2"
			18	1-1/2" x 1-1/2"
			19	2-1/2" x 1-1/2"
			21a	1-1/2" x 1-1/2"
			26	1-1/2" x 1-1/2"

Subcutting, cont.

Fabric		Strip Width	Pc #	Size
Near horse neck & rump	▨	10-1/2"	14	5-1/2" x 10-1/2"
			32	4-1/2" x 6-1/2"
			33	2-1/2" x 7-1/2"
		2-1/2"	15a	2-1/2" x 2-1/2"
		1-1/2"	23	1-1/2" x 2-1/2"
			31a	1-1/2" x 1-1/2"
Near horse mane & tail	▪	3-1/2"	2	3-1/2" x 1-1/2"
			14a	3-1/2" x 3-1/2"
			22	1-1/2" x 2-1/2"
Near horse belly	▨	6-1/2"	35	1-1/2" x 6-1/2"
Near horse collar & hooves	▪	4-1/2"	14c	4-1/2" x 4-1/2"
			15	5-1/2" x 2-1/2"
			24	3-1/2" x 3-1/2"
			31	4-1/2" x 5-1/2"
			28	3-1/2" x 1-1/2"
		1-1/2"	11	1-1/2" x 1-1/2"
			12	1-1/2" x 1-1/2"
			13a	1-1/2" x 1-1/2"
			17	1-1/2" x 1-1/2"
			20	2-1/2" x 1-1/2"
			22a	1-1/2" x 1-1/2"
			29a,b	1-1/2" x 1-1/2"

SEWING

1. 45 Flip - 2a, 5a, 5b, 8a, 8b, 13a, 14c, 15a, 16a, 16b, 21a, 22a, 24a, 28a, 28b, 29a, 29b, 31a, 33a.
2. Piggyback Flip - 14a, 14b.
3. 45 Joint - 19 to 20 to 21, 22 to 23, 31 to 32.
4. Half Square - 12 to 12a, 18 to 18a.
5. Sew 1 thru 34 together as shown to complete Unit B.

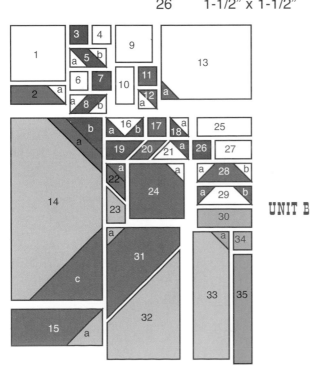

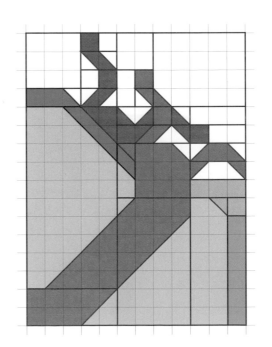

UNIT B

48

RUMPS - UNIT C

SUBCUTTING

Fabric		Strip Width	Pc #	Size
Background	☐	7-1/2"	1	19-1/2" x 7-1/2"
			9	7-1/2" x 2-1/2"
		2-1/2"	10e	2-1/2" x 2-1/2"
			11a	2-1/2" x 2-1/2"
			14	2-1/2" x 2-1/2"
		1-1/2"	3	1-1/2" x 1-1/2"
			5a	1-1/2" x 1-1/2"
			12	1-1/2" x 10-1/2"
Far horse body	▨	4-1/2"	5	4-1/2" x 3-1/2"
		2-1/2"	4	2-1/2" x 2-1/2"
			7	6-1/2" x 2-1/2"
		1-1/2"	10a	1-1/2" x 1-1/2"
Far horse mane & tail	▨	2-1/2"	8	4-1/2" x 2-1/2"
Near horse neck & rump	▨	10-1/2"	10	10-1/2" x 12-1/2"
Near horse mane & tail	▨	3-1/2"	10b	2-1/2" x 2-1/2"
			10f	2-1/2" x 2-1/2"
			11	2-1/2" x 10-1/2"
			13	1-1/2" x 2-1/2"
			14a	1-1/2" x 1-1/2"
Near horse belly	▨	6-1/2"	6	6-1/2" x 11-1/2"
			10c	3-1/2" x 3-1/2"
Near horse face & legs	☐	5-1/2"	10d	3-1/2" x 3-1/2"
Near horse collar & hooves	■	1-1/2"	2	1-1/2" x 1-1/2"

SEWING

1. 45 Flip - 5a, 10a, 10b, 11a, 14a.

2. Half Square Flip - Make a Half Square from 10c
   and 10d and one from 10e and 10f.
   45 Flip these Half Squares to 10.

3. 45 Joint - 7 to 8 to 9.

4. Sew 1 thru 14 together as shown to complete Unit C.

UNIT C

49

FRONT LEGS - UNIT D

SUBCUTTING

Fabric		Strip Width	Pc #	Size
Background	☐	8-1/2"	1	8-1/2" x 18-1/2"
		7-1/2"	6	4-1/2" x 7-1/2"
		2-1/2"	2a	2-1/2" x 2-1/2"
			3a,b	2-1/2" x 2-1/2"
			5	2-1/2" x 3-1/2"
		1-1/2"	4a	1-1/2" x 1-1/2"
Far horse body	▧	4-1/2"	2	4-1/2" x 4-1/2"
			3	4-1/2" x 4-1/2"
			4	2-1/2" x 3-1/2"
			6a	3-1/2" x 3-1/2"
		1-1/2"	5a	1-1/2" x 1-1/2"
Near horse collar & hooves	▨	1-1/2"	2b	1-1/2" x 1-1/2"

SEWING

1. 45 Flip - 2a, 2b, 3a, 3b, 4a, 5a, 6a.
2. Sew 1 thru 6 together as shown to complete Unit D.

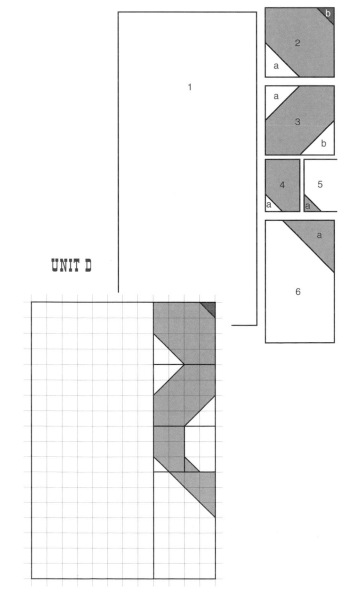

UNIT D

FRONT LEGS - UNIT E

SUBCUTTING

Fabric		Strip width	Pc #	Size
Background	☐	8-1/2"	13	4-1/2" x 3-1/2"
		7-1/2"	24	2-1/2" x 6-1/2"
		2-1/2"	3a,c	2-1/2" x 2-1/2"
			6	3-1/2" x 2-1/2"
			7a	2-1/2" x 2-1/2"
			9	2-1/2" x 2-1/2"
			12	2-1/2" x 3-1/2"
			16a	2-1/2" x 2-1/2"
			17	3-1/2" x 2-1/2"
			23	2-1/2" x 2-1/2"
		1-1/2"	11c	1-1/2" x 1-1/2"
			15	2-1/2" x 1-1/2"
			19	1-1/2" x 1-1/2"
			20a	1-1/2" x 1-1/2"
			22	1-1/2" x 2-1/2"
			25a,b	1-1/2" x 1-1/2"
			26a	1-1/2" x 1-1/2"
			27	1-1/2" x 2-1/2"
Far horse body	▧	4-1/2"	7	3-1/2" x 2-1/2"
			20	2-1/2" x 4-1/2"
		2-1/2"	1a	2-1/2" x 2-1/2"
			21	1-1/2" x 2-1/2"
		1-1/2"	3b	1-1/2" x 1-1/2"
			10a	1-1/2" x 1-1/2"
			11a	1-1/2" x 1-1/2"
			15a	1-1/2" x 1-1/2"
Far horse collar & hooves	▨	3-1/2"	11	2-1/2" x 2-1/2"
			21a	1-1/2" x 1-1/2"

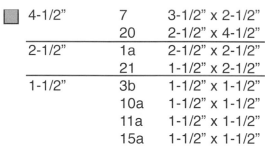
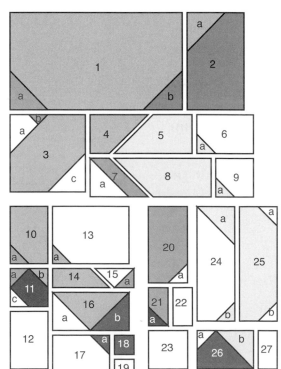

UNIT E

Unit E Subcutting, cont.

Fabric	Strip width	Pc #	Size
Near horse neck & rump	▨ 10-1/2"	1	9-1/2" x 5-1/2"
		3	4-1/2" x 4-1/2"
	2-1/2"	2a	2-1/2" x 2-1/2"
		4	3-1/2" x 2-1/2"
		10	2-1/2" x 3-1/2"
		16	4-1/2" x 2-1/2"
	1-1/2"	11b	1-1/2" x 1-1/2"
		13a	1-1/2" x 1-1/2"
		14	3-1/2" x 1-1/2"
Near horse belly	▨ 6-1/2"	1b	2-1/2" x 2-1/2"
		2	3-1/2" x 5-1/2"
Near horse face & legs	☐ 5-1/2"	5	4-1/2" x 2-1/2"
		8	5-1/2" x 2-1/2"
		24a	2-1/2" x 2-1/2"
		25	2-1/2" x 6-1/2"
		26b	2-1/2" x 2-1/2"
	1-1/2"	6a	1-1/2" x 1-1/2"
		9a	1-1/2" x 1-1/2"
		24b	1-1/2" x 1-1/2"
Near horse collar & hooves	▨ 4-1/2"	16b	2-1/2" x 2-1/2"
		26	3-1/2" x 2-1/2"
	1-1/2"	17a	1-1/2" x 1-1/2"
		18	1-1/2" x 1-1/2"

SEWING

1. 45 Flip - 1a, 1b, 2a, 3c, 6a, 7a, 9a, 10a, 11a, 11b, 11c, 13a, 15a, 16a, 16b, 17a, 20a, 21a, 24a, 24b, 25a, 25b, 26a, 26b.
2. Flips in Order - Flip 3b onto 3a, Flip this onto 3.
3. 45 Joint - 4 to 5, 7 to 8, 14 to 15.
4. Sew 1 thru 27 together as shown to complete Unit E.

REAR FEET - UNIT F
SUBCUTTING

Fabric	Strip Width	Pc #	Size
Background	☐ 8-1/2"	1	7-1/2" x 8-1/2"
		11	8-1/2" x 2-1/2"
	2-1/2"	7	2-1/2" x 4-1/2"
		8	4-1/2" x 2-1/2"
		10	4-1/2" x 2-1/2"
	1-1/2"	3b	1-1/2" x 1-1/2"
		6a	1-1/2" x 1-1/2"
		9a	1-1/2" x 1-1/2"
		12a	1-1/2" x 1-1/2"
Far horse body	▨ 2-1/2"	1a,c	2-1/2" x 2-1/2"
		3	2-1/2" x 7-1/2"
		9b	2-1/2" x 2-1/2"
	1-1/2"	4a	1-1/2" x 1-1/2"
		5	1-1/2" x 1-1/2"
		7a	1-1/2" x 1-1/2"
Far horse collar & hooves	▨ 3-1/2"	9	3-1/2" x 2-1/2"
Near horse neck & rump	▨ 2-1/2"	4	2-1/2" x 3-1/2"
		10a	2-1/2" x 2-1/2"
		12b	2-1/2" x 2-1/2"
	1-1/2"	6	1-1/2" x 1-1/2"
Near horse face & legs	☐ 1-1/2"	1b	1-1/2" x 1-1/2"
		2	2-1/2" x 1-1/2"
		3a	1-1/2" x 1-1/2"
Near horse collar & hooves	▨ 4-1/2"	12	3-1/2" x 2-1/2"

SEWING

1. 45 Flip - 1c, 3a, 3b, 4a, 7a, 9a, 9b, 10a, 12a, 12b.
2. Piggyback Flip - 1a, 1b.
3. Half Square - 6a to 6.
4. Sew 1 thru 12 together as shown to complete Unit F.

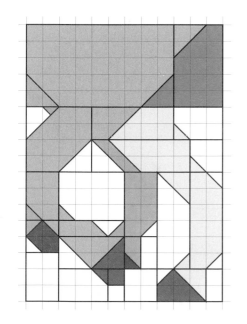

UNIT E

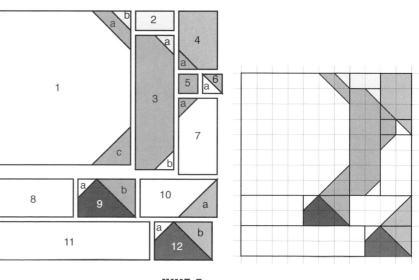

UNIT F

REAR LEGS - UNIT G

SUBCUTTING

Fabric	Strip Width	Pc #	Size
Background ☐	8-1/2"	14	8-1/2" x 2-1/2"
		7	3-1/2" x 3-1/2"
	2-1/2"	2	2-1/2" x 2-1/2"
		3b	1-1/2" x 2-1/2"
		8b	2-1/2" x 2-1/2"
		11	2-1/2" x 3-1/2"
		12b	2-1/2" x 2-1/2"
	1-1/2"	1a	1-1/2" x 1-1/2"
		5	1-1/2" x 1-1/2"
		6a	1-1/2" x 1-1/2"
		8a	1-1/2" x 1-1/2"
		9	1-1/2" x 3-1/2"
		13	3-1/2" x 1-1/2"
Far horse body ▧	1-1/2"	3c	1-1/2" x 1-1/2"
Far horse collar & hooves ■	3-1/2"	1b	1-1/2" x 1-1/2"
		3a	1-1/2" x 2-1/2"
		4	1-1/2" x 1-1/2"
Near horse neck & rump ▨	10-1/2"	1	3-1/2" x 7-1/2"
	2-1/2"	6	2-1/2" x 3-1/2"
Near horse mane & tail ■	3-1/2"	8	2-1/2" x 3-1/2"
Near horse face & legs ☐	5-1/2"	3	2-1/2" x 4-1/2"
		12	3-1/2" x 3-1/2"
	1-1/2"	2a	1-1/2" x 1-1/2"
		8c	1-1/2" x 1-1/2"
		10	1-1/2" x 3-1/2"
		11a	1-1/2" x 1-1/2"
Near horse collar & hooves ■	4-1/2"	12a	3-1/2" x 3-1/2"

SEWING

1. 45 Flip - 2a, 6a, 8a, 11a.
2. Piggyback Flip - 8b, 8c.
3. Half Square Flip - Sew the 1a and 1b pieces into a Half Square, 45 Flip this to 1. Sew 12 and 12a into a Half Square; 45 Flip 12b to it.
4. Half Strip Flip - Sew 3a and 3b together as a Half Strip; sew 3c on as a 45 Flip. Use this whole set as the flip for Piece 3.

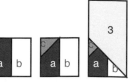

5. Sew 1 thru 14 together as shown to complete Unit G.

QUILT ASSEMBLY

Sew Unit A left of Unit B and Unit D left of Unit E. Sew A-B above D-E. Sew Unit F left of Unit G. Sew Unit C above F-G. Sew ABDE left of CFG.

INNER BORDER CUTTING

Fabric	# of Strips	Strip Width
Background	5	1-1/2"
Inner Border	5	1-1/2"
Outer Border	5	4-1/2"

SEWING

1. Sew each background strip to a inner border strip, lengthwise.
2. Cut eight 1-1/2" segments from one of these strip sets.
3. Make four 4-patch with the segments.
4. Measure the width and length of the quilt. Cut two side borders and a top and bottom border from the strip sets, piecing as necessary. Sew on the side borders.
5. Sew a 4-patch to each end of the remaining borders. Sew these to the top and bottom.
6. Sew on the 4-1/2" outer border, joining strips as necessary.

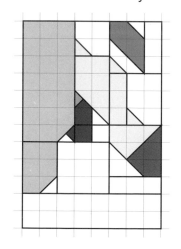

UNIT G

2.

3.

BUTTERCUP AND BABY
36" X 32"
PG.41

ART
AND THE
CHICKENS
55" X 45"
PG.20

THE MICE
15" X 8"
PG. 104

WHEN YOU WISH UPON A STAR
31" X 27"
PG. 100

I DARE YOU
43" X 22"
PG. 95

CODY
AND HIS
GIRLS
45" X 28"
PG.9

WILD
GOOSE
CHASE
52" X 34"
PG. 70

WHEN PIGS FLY...BY NIGHT!
24" X 20"
PG. 92

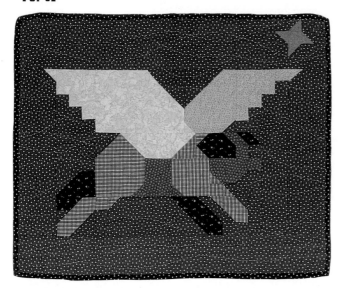

CHARLOTTE AND WILBUR
24" X 24"
PG. 89

THREE LITTLE PIGS
53" X 41"   PG. 82

YAHOO
40" X 36"
PG. 76

TICK TALK
48" X 36"
PG. 14

BELLE AND BUDDY
44" X 41"
PG. 61

FRED AND
SONNY
55" X 45"
PG. 46

60

BELLE ᴀɴᴅ BUDDY

44" x 41"

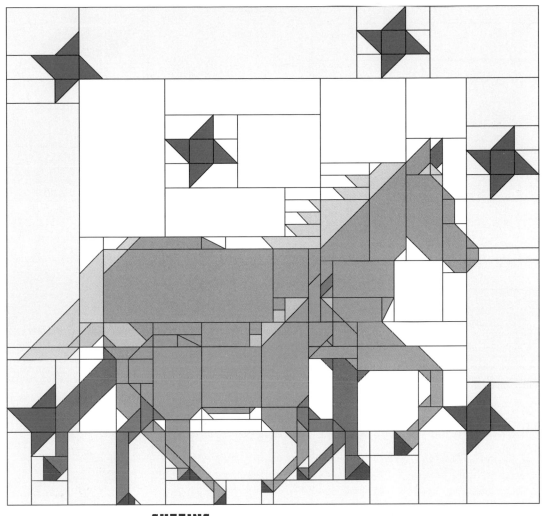

YARDAGE

3/4 yd.	☐	Background
1/2 yd.	▨	Mare body
1/8 yd.	▨	Mare far legs & ear
1/4 yd.	☐	Mare mane & tail
1/8 yd.	▨	Mare hooves
1/4 yd.	▨	Foal body
1/8 yd.	▨	Foal far legs & ear
1/8 yd.	☐	Foal mane & tail
1/8 yd.	▨	Foal hooves
7/8 yd.	☐	Border
1/2 yd.		Binding
2-5/8 yds.		Backing

Assorted Scraps for six 6"
(finished) Star Blocks ▨

CUTTING

Cut all strips crosswise as shown in Rotary Cutting. Cut the following strips, then refer to each Unit's cutting chart for size of pieces to cut from each strip. Pieces may be subcut from a wider strip.

Fabric		# of Strips	Strip Width
Background	☐	1	7-1/2"
		1	4-1/2"
		2	2-1/2"
		1	1-1/2"
Mare body	▨	1	6-1/2"
		1	3-1/2"
		1	2-1/2"
		1	1-1/2"
Mare far legs & ear	▨	1	3-1/2"

Cutting, cont.

Fabric		# of Strips	Strip Width
Mare mane & tail	☐	1	4-1/2"
		1	1-1/2"
Mare hooves	▨	1	2-1/2"
Foal body	▨	1	5-1/2"
		1	1-1/2"
Foal far legs & ear	▨	1	2-1/2"
Foal mane & tail	☐	1	2-1/2"
Foal hooves	▨	1	1-1/2"
Border	☐	2	6-1/2"
		2	4-1/2"
		2	2-1/2"

MARE BACK - UNIT A

SUBCUTTING

Fabric		Strip Width	Pc#	Size
Background	☐	7-1/2"	1	7-1/2" x 13-1/2"
			4	7-1/2" x 6-1/2"
		4-1/2"	2	13-1/2" x 3-1/2"
			5	10-1/2" x 4-1/2"
		2-1/2"	3 (cut 2)	4-1/2" x 2-1/2"
			(cut 4)	2-1/2" x 2-1/2"
			8	2-1/2" x 1-1/2"
			11	2-1/2" x 3-1/2"
			13	2-1/2" x 1-1/2"
			16a	2-1/2" x 1-1/2"
		1-1/2"	6	3-1/2" x 1-1/2"
			7	3-1/2" x 1-1/2"
			10a	1-1/2" x 1-1/2"
			17	4-1/2" x 1-1/2"
Mare body	▨	6-1/2"	15	6-1/2" x 1-1/2"
			19	14-1/2" x 6-1/2"
		3-1/2"	20	3-1/2" x 4-1/2"
			24	1-1/2" x 3-1/2"
		2-1/2"	16	2-1/2" x 1-1/2"
		1-1/2"	21	1-1/2" x 1-1/2"
Mare mane & tail	▨	4-1/2"	12	2-1/2" x 6-1/2"
			19a	2-1/2" x 2-1/2"
		1-1/2"	7a	1-1/2" x 1-1/2"
			9	2-1/2" x 1-1/2"
			10	3-1/2" x 1-1/2"
			14	2-1/2" x 1-1/2"
			18	5-1/2" x 1-1/2"
Foal body	▨	5-1/2"	23	2-1/2" x 2-1/2"
			25	1-1/2" x 4-1/2"
Foal mane & tail	▨	2-1/2"	22	1-1/2" x 1-1/2"
			23a	2-1/2" x 2-1/2"
Star	▨	Scraps	3a (cut 5)	2-12" x 2-1/2"

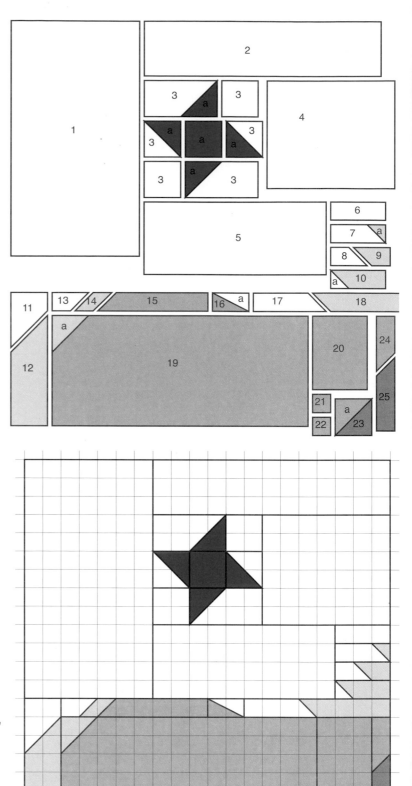

UNIT A

STAR BLOCK

Sew the Star Block using 3 and 3a pieces in 45 Flips and Half Squares. See illustration above right.

SEWING

1. 45 Flip - 7a, 10a, 19a.
2. 45 Joint - 8 to 9, 11 to 12, 13 to 14 to 15, 17 to 18, 24 to 25.
3. Half Square - 23 and 23a.
4. Half Rectangle - 16 and 16a.
5. Sew 1 thru 25 together as shown to complete Unit A.

MARE HEAD - UNIT B

SUBCUTTING

Fabric		Strip Width	Pc #	Size
Background	☐	7-1/2"	1	7-1/2" x 7-1/2"
			9	5-1/2" x 5-1/2"
		4-1/2"	2	4-1/2" x 1-1/2"
			23	4-1/2" x 5-1/2"
			25	2-1/2" x 4-1/2"
		2-1/2"	5	2-1/2" x 1-1/2"
			10a	2-1/2" x 2-1/2"
			12b	2-1/2" x 2-1/2"
			13	2-1/2" x 5-1/2"
			15	1-1/2" x 2-1/2"
			22a	1-1/2" x 2-1/2"
			24a	1-1/2" x 1-1/2"
		1-1/2"	3	3-1/2" x 1-1/2"
			8b,c	1-1/2" x 1-1/2"
			11a,b	1-1/2" x 1-1/2"
			16a	1-1/2" x 1-1/2"
Mare body	▨	6-1/2"	7	4-1/2" x 5-1/2"
			20	5-1/2" x 3-1/2"
			21	4-1/2" x 2-1/2"
		3-1/2"	8	3-1/2" x 8-1/2"
			10	2-1/2" x 3-1/2"
			12	3-1/2" x 7-1/2"
			16	2-1/2" x 3-1/2"
		2-1/2"	14	1-1/2" x 2-1/2"
			17	1-1/2" x 2-1/2"
			22	1-1/2" x 2-1/2"
		1-1/2"	13a	1-1/2" x 1-1/2"
			18a	1-1/2" x 1-1/2"
			24	2-1/2" x 1-1/2"
Mare far legs & ear	▨	3-1/2"	11	1-1/2" x 3-1/2"
Mare mane & tail	☐	4-1/2"	7a	4-1/2" x 4-1/2"
			8a	3-1/2" x 3-1/2"
		1-1/2"	4	2-1/2" x 1-1/2"
			6	3-1/2" x 1-1/2"
			10b	1-1/2" x 1-1/2"
			11c	1-1/2" x 1-1/2"
			12a	1-1/2" x 1-1/2"
Foal body	▨	5-1/2"	19	1-1/2" x 2-1/2"
		1-1/2"	21a	1-1/2" x 1-1/2"
Foal far legs & ear	▨	2-1/2"	18	1-1/2" x 2-1/2"
Foal mane & tail	☐	2-1/2"	19a	1-1/2" x 1-1/2"

SEWING

1. 45 Flip - 7a, 8c, 10a, 10b, 11a, 12a, 12b, 13a, 16a, 18a, 19a, 21a, 24a.
2. Flips in Order - 11b and 11c.
3. Piggyback Flip - 8a, 8b.
4. 45 Joint - 3 to 4, 5 to 6, 17 to 18.
5. Half Rectangle - 22 and 22a.
6. Sew 1 thru 25 together as shown to complete Unit B.

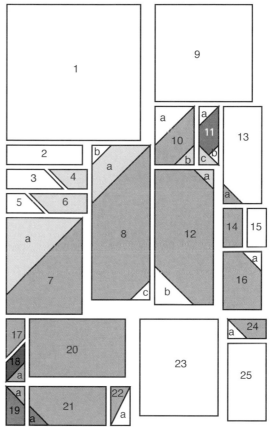

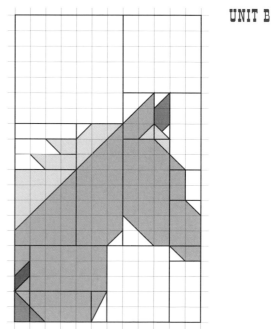

UNIT B

63

MARE & FOAL BODIES - UNIT C

SUBCUTTING

Fabric		Strip Width	Pc #	Size
Background	☐	4-1/2"	7	3-1/2" x 4-1/2"
			24a	4-1/2" x 1"
		2-1/2"	2	2-1/2" x 1-1/2"
			6a	2-1/2" x 2-1/2"
			10b	2-1/2" x 2-1/2"
		1-1/2"	1b	1-1/2" x 1-1/2"
			16b	1-1/2" x 1-1/2"
			17a	1-1/2" x 1-1/2"
			19	1-1/2" x 1-1/2"
			24b	1-1/2" x 1-1/2"
			25	1-1/2" x 1-1/2"
			26	5-1/2" x 1-1/2"
			28a	1-1/2" x 1-1/2"
Mare body	▨	6-1/2"	13	4-1/2" x 1-1/2"
		3-1/2"	4	3-1/2" x 1-1/2"
		2-1/2"	3b	2-1/2" x 2-1/2"
			10	2-1/2" x 4-1/2"
			20	4-1/2" x 2-1/2"
		1-1/2"	3a	1-1/2" x 1-1/2"
			8	1-1/2" x 2-1/2"
			12a	1-1/2" x 1-1/2"
			15a	2-1/2" x 1-1/2"
			17	1-1/2" x 1-1/2"
			21	1-1/2" x 1-1/2"
Mare far legs & ear	▨	3-1/2"	4a	1-1/2" x 1-1/2"
			6	3-1/2" x 5-1/2"
Mare mane & tail	▨	1-1/2"	1a	1 1/2" x 1-1/2"

Cutting, cont.

Fabric		Strip Width	Pc #	Size
Foal body	▨	5-1/2"	5	2-1/2" x 1-1/2"
			9	2-1/2" x 2-1/2"
			11	1-1/2" x 2-1/2"
			14	2-1/2" x 1-1/2"
			16	4-1/2" x 6-1/2"
			23	5-1/2" x 5-1/2"
			27	4-1/2" x 7-1/2"
			28	3-1/2" x 2-1/2"
		1-1/2"	3c	1-1/2" x 1-1/2"
			10a	1-1/2" x 1-1/2"
			15	2-1/2" x 1-1/2"
			18	2-1/2" x 1-1/2"
			24	4-1/2" x 1"
			25a	1" x 1"
			29a	1-1/2" x 1-1/2"
Foal far legs & ear	▨	2-1/2"	10c	2-1/2" x 2-1/2"
			12	1-1/2" x 3-1/2"
			16a	1-1/2" x 1-1/2"
			27b	1-1/2" x 1-1/2"
			29	1-1/2" x 2-1/2"
Foal mane & tail	▨	2-1/2"	1	2-1/2" x 2-1/2"
			3	4-1/2" x 2-1/2"
			22	1-1/2" x 1-1/2"
			27a	2-1/2" x 2-1/2"

SEWING

1. 45 Flip - 1a,1b, 3a, 4a, 6a, 10a, 12a, 16a, 16b, 17a, 25a, 27a, 27b, 28a, 29a.
2. Flips in Order - 3b and 3c, 10b and 10c.
3. 45 Joints - 4 to 5, 6 to 7, 11 to 12.
4. Half Rectangle - 15 and 15a.
5. Half Strip - Sew 24 and 24a together. Add 24b as a 45 Flip.
6. Sew 1 thru 29 together as shown to complete Unit C.

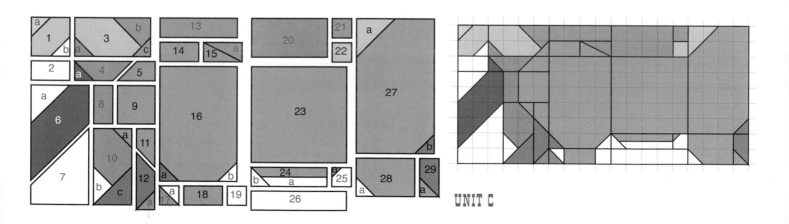

UNIT C

MARE FRONT LEGS – UNIT D

SUBCUTTING

Fabric		Strip Width	Pc #	Size
Background	☐	7-1/2"	11	5-1/2" x 5-1/2"
		2-1/2"	4	2-1/2" x 5-1/2"
			8	7-1/2" x 2-1/2"
			10	4-1/2" x 2-1/2"
			12	1-1/2" x 3-1/2"
			14	2-1/2" x 3-1/2"
			15	4-1/2" x 2-1/2"
Mare body	▨	6-1/2"	3	4-1/2" x 1-1/2"
		3-1/2"	13	1-1/2" x 3-1/2"
		2-1/2"	7	4-1/2" x 2-1/2"
			9	7-1/2" x 2-1/2"
			15a	2-1/2" x 2-1/2"
		1-1/2"	1b	1-1/2" x 1-1/2"
			2a	1-1/2" x 1-1/2"
			6a	1-1/2" x 1-1/2"
			11b	1-1/2" x 1-1/2"
			12a,b	1-1/2" x 1-1/2"
Mare far legs & ear	▨	3-1/2"	4a	1-1/2" x 1-1/2"
			6	2-1/2" x 6-1/2"
			11a	1-1/2" x 1-1/2"
Foal body	▨	5-1/2"	1	2-1/2" x 2-1/2"
			2	2-1/2" x 2-1/2"
		1-1/2"	1a	1-1/2" x 1-1/2"
			3a	1-1/2" x 1-1/2"
Foal far legs & ear	▨	2-1/2"	4b	1-1/2" x 1-1/2"
			5	2-1/2" x 1-1/2"
			6b	1-1/2" x 1-1/2"
Star	▪	Scraps	15b	2-1/2" x 2 1/2"

SEWING

1. 45 Flip - 2a, 3a, 4a, 4b, 6a, 6b, 11a, 11b, 12a, 12b, 15a, 15b.

2. 45 Joint - 7 to 8, 9 to 10.

3. Half Square Flip - Make a Half Square of 1a and 1b. Use as a 45 Flip on 1.

4. Sew 1 thru 15 together as shown to complete Unit D.

ASSEMBLY
Sew Unit A to Unit B and Unit C to Unit D. Sew A-B to C-D. The Inner section is complete.

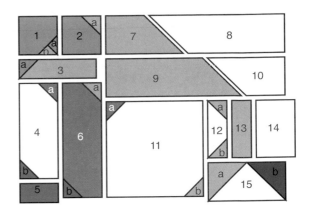

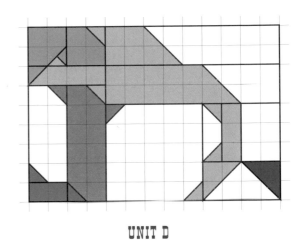

UNIT D

Uncle John Melvon "Casey" Jones and Capitan. Cap was so smart that he learned to open the feed bins and help himself.

LEFT BORDER

SUBCUTTING

Fabric		Strip Width	Pc #	Size
Border	☐	6-1/2"	3	6-1/2" x 20-1/2"
		4-1/2"	1	4-1/2" x 2-1/2"
			6	4-1/2" x 4-1/2"
			8	2-1/2" x 4-1/2"
		2-1/2"	2a	2-1/2" x 2-1/2"
			4	2-1/2" x 1-1/2"
			5a	1-1/2" x 1-1/2"
			7a	2-1/2" x 2-1/2"
			9a	1-1/2" x 1-1/2"
Star	■	Scraps	2	2-1/2" x 2-1/2"
			6a	2-1/2" x 2-1/2"
			7	4-1/2" x 2-1/2"
Mare body	▨	3-1/2"	9	2-1/2" x 4-1/2"
Mare mane & tail	▨	4-1/2"	3a	4-1/2" x 4-1/2"
		1-1/2"	5	5-1/2" x 1-1/2"
Foal mane & tail	▨	2-1/2"	3b	1-1/2" x 1-1/2"

SEWING

1. 45 flip - 5a, 6a, 7a, 9a.
2. Piggyback Flip - 3a, 3b.
3. 45 Joint - 4 to 5, 8 to 9.
3. Half Square - 2 to 2a.
4. Sew 1 thru 9 together as shown to complete Border 1.

RIGHT BORDER

SUBCUTTING

Fabric		Strip Width	Pc #	Size
Border	☐	6-1/2"	5	5-1/2" x 1-1/2"
			6	6-1/2" x 10-1/2"
		4-1/2"	1	6-1/2" x 4-1/2"
			2 (cut 2)	4-1/2" x 2-1/2"
			3	6-1/2" x 4-1/2"
			8	4-1/2" x 4-1/2"
		2-1/2"	2 (cut 4)	2-1/2" x 2-1/2"
			7a	2-1/2" x 2-1/2"
Star	■	Scraps	2a (cut 5)	2-1/2" x 2-1/2"
			7	2-1/2" x 4-1/2"
			8a	2-1/2" x 2-1/2"
Mare body	▨	1-1/2"	3a	1-1/2" x 1-1/2"
			4	1-1/2" x 1-1/2"
			6a	1-1/2" x 1-1/2"

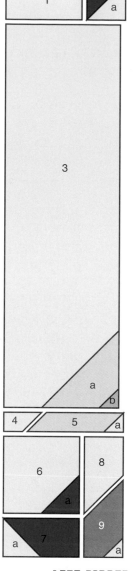
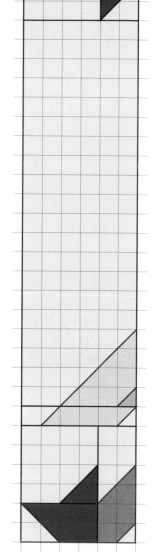

LEFT BORDER

Right Border, cont.

SEWING

1. Sew the Star Block using the 2 and 2a pieces and 45 Flips and Half Squares, as shown below.
2. 45 Flip - 3a, 6a, 7a, 8a.
3. Sew 1 thru 8 together as shown to complete Border 2.

TOP BORDER

SUBCUTTING

Fabric		Strip Width	Pc #	Size
Border		6-1/2"	4	23-1/2" x 6-1/2"
			6	9-1/2" x 6-1/2"
		4-1/2"	1	6-1/2" x 4-1/2"
			2	4-1/2" x 2-1/2"
		2-1/2"	5(cut 2)	4-1/2" x 2-1/2"
			(cut 4)	2-1/2" x 2-1/2"
Star		Scraps	1a	2-1/2" x 2-1/2"
			3	4-1/2" x 2-1/2"
			4a	2-1/2" x 2-1/2"
			5a (cut 5)	2-1/2" x 2-1/2"

SEWING

1. Sew the Star Block using the 5 and 5a pieces and 45 Flips and Half Squares, as shown above.
2. 45 Flip - 1a, 4a.
3. 45 Joint - 2 to 3.
4. Sew 1 thru 6 together as shown to complete Border 3.

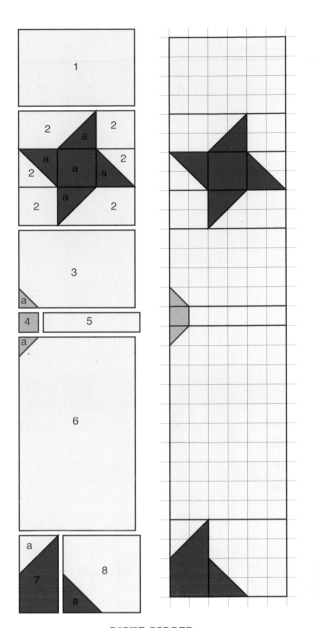

RIGHT BORDER

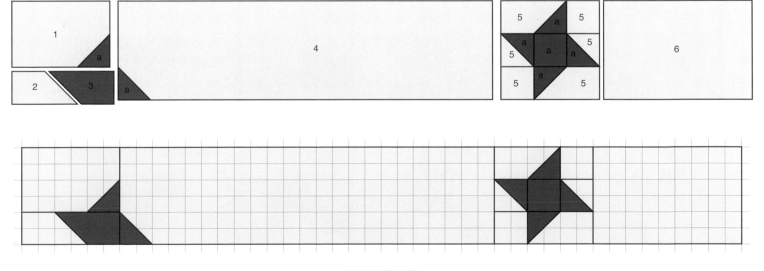

TOP BORDER

LEGS & HOOVES - BOTTOM BORDER

SUBCUTTING

Fabric		Strip Width	Pc #	Size
Border	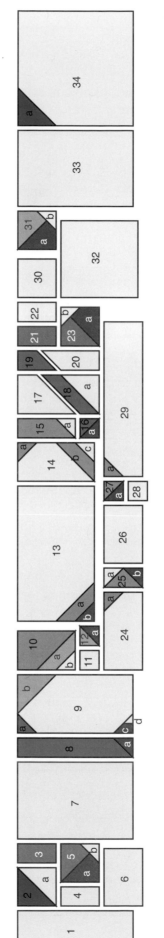	6-1/2"	1	2-1/2" x 6-1/2"
			9	3-1/2" x 6-1/2"
			34	6-1/2" x 6-1/2"
		4-1/2"	6	3-1/2" x 2-1/2"
			7	4-1/2" x 6-1/2"
			13	7-1/2" x 4-1/2"
			14	2-1/2" x 4-1/2"
			17	2-1/2" x 3-1/2"
			24	4-1/2" x 2-1/2"
			26	3-1/2" x 2-1/2"
			32	4-1/2" x 4-1/2"
			33	4-1/2" x 6-1/2"
		2-1/2"	2a	2-1/2" x 2-1/2"
			4	1-1/2" x 2-1/2"
			5b	1-1/2" x 1-1/2"
			9d	1" x 1-1/2"
			10b	1-1/2" x 1-1/2"
			11	1-1/2" x 1-1/2"
			14c	1-1/2" x 1-1/2"
			15a	1-1/2" x 1-1/2"
			18a	2-1/2" x 2-1/2"
			20	1-1/2" x 3-1/2"
			22	1-1/2" x 2-1/2"
			23b	1-1/2" x 1-1/2"
			25a	1-1/2" x 1-1/2"
			28	1-1/2" x 1-1/2"
			29	8-1/2" x 2-1/2"
			30	2-1/2" x 2-1/2"
			31b	1-1/2" x 1-1/2"
Mare body		2-1/2"	9b	2-1/2" x 2-1/2"
			10a	2-1/2" x 2-1/2"
			31	2-1/2" x 2-1/2"
		1-1/2"	12	1-1/2" x 1-1/2"
Mare far legs & ear		3-1/2"	3	1-1/2" x 2-1/2"
			5	2-1/2" x 2-1/2"
			21	1-1/2" x 2-1/2"
			23	2-1/2" x 2-1/2"
Mare hooves		2-1/2"	5a	2-1/2" x 2-1/2"
			12a	1-1/2" x 1-1/2"
			13b	1-1/2" x 1-1/2"
			23a	2-1/2" x 2-1/2"
			31a	2-1/2" x 2-1/2"

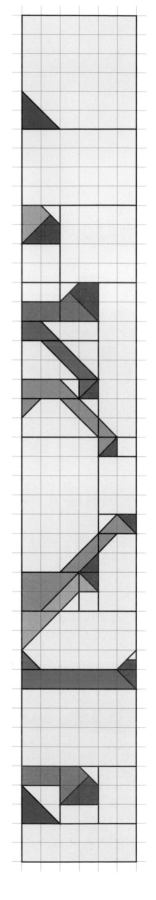

BOTTOM BORDER

Subcutting, cont.

Fabric		Strip Width	Pc #	Size
Foal body	■	5-1/2"	10	2-1/2" x 3-1/2"
			13a	2-1/2" x 2-1/2"
			14b	2-1/2" x 2-1/2"
		1-1/2"	14a	1-1/2" x 1-1/2"
			15	1-1/2" x 3-1/2"
			24a	1-1/2" x 1-1/2"
			25	1-1/2" x 2-1/2"
			27	1-1/2" x 1-1/2"
			29a	1-1/2" x 1-1/2"
Foal far legs & ear	■	2-1/2"	8	1-1/2" x 6-1/2"
			9a	1-1/2" x 1-1/2"
			16	1-1/2" x 1-1/2"
			18	2-1/2" x 3-1/2"
			19	1-1/2" x 2-1/2"
Foal hooves	■	1-1/2"	8a	1-1/2" x 1-1/2"
			9c	1" x 1-1/2"
			16a	1-1/2" x 1-1/2"
			25b	1-1/2" x 1-1/2"
			27a	1-1/2" x 1-1/2"
Star	■	Scraps	2	2-1/2" x 2-1/2"
			34a	2-1/2" x 2-1/2"

SEWING

1. 45 Flip - 8a, 9a, 9b, 14a, 15a, 18a, 24a, 25a, 25b, 29a, 34a.

2. Piggyback Flip - 10a, 10b; 13a, 13b; 14b, 14c.

3. Half Square - Make a Half Square with 2 and 2a; 5 and 5a, flip 5b to it; 12 and 12a; 16 and 16a; 23 and 23a, flip 23b to it; 27 and 27a; 31 and 31a, flip 31b to it.

4. 45 Joint - 17 to 18, 19 to 20.

5. Half Strip Flip - Sew 9c to 9d. Use as a flip on 9.

6. Sew 1 thru 34 together as shown to complete Border 4.

ASSEMBLY

Sew Borders 1 and 2 to the sides of the Inner Section. Sew Borders 3 and 4 to top and bottom.

The girls went back and forth to town in their one-horse cart. Town and school were across the river, one mile away.

WILD GOOSE CHASE
52" x 34"

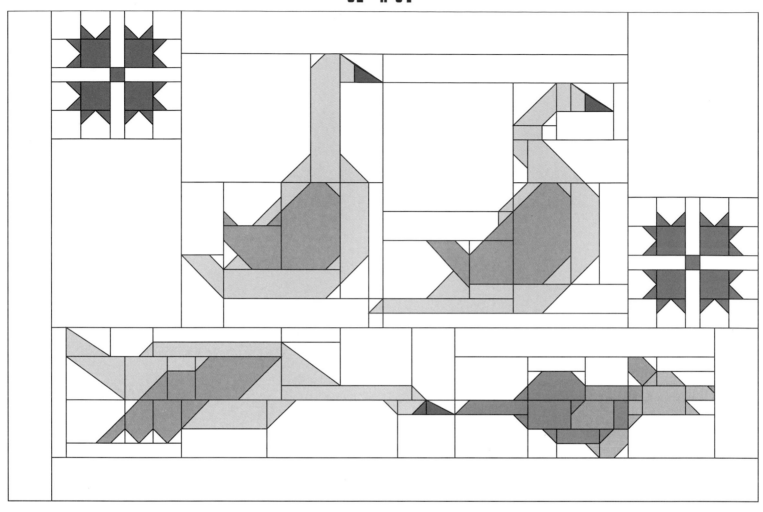

Designed by Holly Rogers
Steamboat Springs, Colorado

YARDAGE

1-5/8 yds.	Background
1/3 yd.	Goose body
1/4 yd.	Goose wing
Scrap	Beak
1/8 yd.	Dog rear
1/8 yd.	Dog ear & middle
1/8 yd.	Dog head
1/8 yd.	Goose Track
1/2 yd.	Binding
1-2/3 yds.	Backing

CUTTING

Cut all strips cross wise as shown in Rotary Cutting. Cut the following strips, then refer to each Unit's cutting chart for size of pieces to cut from each strip. Pieces may be subcut from a wider strip.

Fabric	# of Strips	Strip Width
Background	2	9-1/2"
	5	3-1/2"
	4	2-1/2"
	4	1-1/2"
Goose body	1	3-1/2"
	2	2-1/2"
	1	1-1/2"

Cutting, cont.

Fabric	# of Strips	Strip Width
Goose wing	1	4-1/2"
	1	2-1/2"
Beak	1	Scrap
Dog rear	1	2-1/2"
Dog ear & middle	1	2-1/2"
Dog head	1	2-1/2"
Goose Tracks	1	2-1/2"
	1	1-1/2"

GANDER - UNIT A

SUBCUTTING

Fabric	Strip Width	Pc #	Size
Background	9-1/2"	1	9-1/2" x 9-1/2"
		4	3-1/2" x 7-1/2"
		5	3-1/2" x 5-1/2"
		6	3-1/2" x 5-1/2"
	3-1/2"	3	3-1/2" x 2-1/2"
		7	4-1/2" x 3-1/2"
		8b	2-1/2" x 2-1/2"
		12	2-1/2" x 3-1/2"
	2-1/2"	13	1-1/2" x 8-1/2"
		14	10-1/2" x 2-1/2"
	1-1/2"	2a	1-1/2" x 1-1/2"
		6b	1-1/2" x 1-1/2"
		10a	1-1/2" x 1-1/2"
		15	1-1/2" x 1-1/2"
		16	1-1/2" x 1-1/2"
Goose body	3-1/2"	6a	3-1/2" x 3-1/2"
		9b,c	1-1/2" x 1-1/2"
		15a	1-1/2" x 1-1/2"
	2-1/2"	1a	2-1/2" x 2-1/2"
		2	2-1/2" x 9-1/2"
		3a	1-1/2" x 2-1/2"
		4a	2-1/2" x 2-1/2"
		7a	2-1/2" x 2-1/2"
		8a	2-1/2" x 2-1/2"
		9a	2-1/2" x 2-1/2"
		10	8-1/2" x 2-1/2"
		11	2-1/2" x 7-1/2"
Goose wing	4-1/2"	7b,c	1-1/2" x 1-1/2"
		8	4-1/2" x 3-1/2"
		9	4-1/2" x 6-1/2"
Beak	Scrap	3b	2-1/2" x 2-1/2"

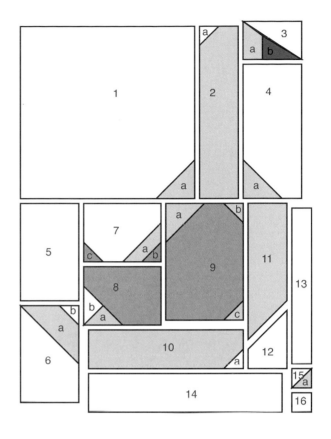

SEWING

1. 45 Flip - 1a, 2a, 4a, 7c, 9a, 9b, 9c, 10a.

2. Piggyback Flip - 6a, 6b; 7a, 7b.

3. Combination Half Rectangle Flip - Sew 3a to 3b. Join 3 and 3ab as a Half Rectangle.

4. Half Square Flip - 8a and 8b, onto 8.

5. Half Square - 15, 15a

6. Sew 1 thru 16 together as shown to complete Unit A.

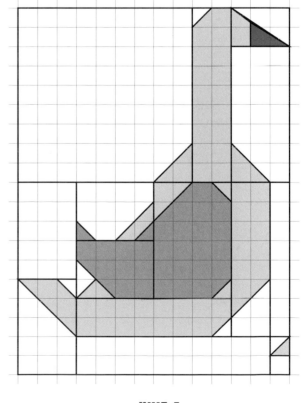

UNIT A

GOOSE - UNIT B

SUBCUTTING

Fabric		Strip Width	Pc #	Size
Background	☐	9-1/2"	1	9-1/2" x 9-1/2"
			3	6-1/2" x 4-1/2"
			17	6-1/2" x 3-1/2"
		3-1/2"	7	3-1/2" x 3-1/2"
			11	3-1/2" x 2-1/2"
			12	4-1/2" x 2-1/2"
			20	2-1/2" x 7-1/2"
		2-1/2"	2	8-1/2" x 2-1/2"
			13	1-1/2" x 4-1/2"
			15	1-1/2" x 2-1/2"
			19b	2-1/2" x 2-1/2"
			22	6-1/2" x 2-1/2"
			24	17-1/2" x 2-1/2"
		1-1/2"	3c	1-1/2" x 1-1/2"
			4a	1-1/2" x 1-1/2"
			7b	1-1/2" x 1-1/2"
			9	1-1/2" x 1-1/2"
			18b	1-1/2" x 1-1/2"
			19a	1-1/2" x 1-1/2"
			23	17-1/2" x 1-1/2"
Goose body	☐	3-1/2"	3a	3-1/2" x 3-1/2"
			5	3-1/2" x 1-1/2"
			7a	3-1/2" x 3-1/2"
			16	4-1/2" x 3-1/2"
		2-1/2"	2a	1-1/2" x 2-1/2"
			8	2-1/2" x 1-1/2"
			10	1-1/2" x 2-1/2"
			11a	1-1/2" x 2-1/2"
			14	1-1/2" x 2-1/2"
			18a,d	2-1/2" x 2-1/2"
			19	2-1/2" x 7-1/2"
			21	4-1/2" x 2-1/2"
		1-1/2"	1a	1-1/2" x 1-1/2"
			6	9-1/2" x 1-1/2"
			18c	1-1/2" x 1-1/2"
Goose wing	▨	4-1/2"	2b	2-1/2" x 2-1/2"
			3b	3-1/2" x 3-1/2"
			4	3-1/2" x 3-1/2"
			18	4-1/2" x 7-1/2"
Beak	■	Scrap	11b	2-1/2" x 2-1/2"

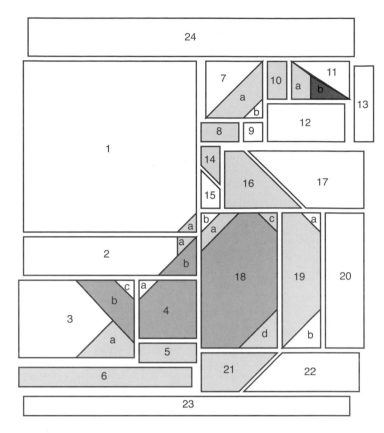

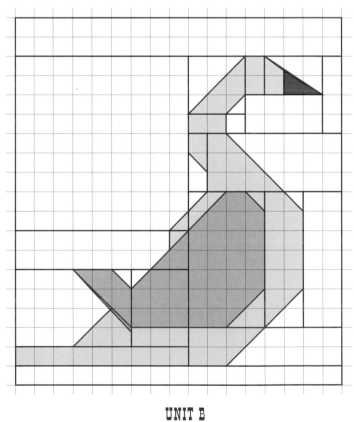

UNIT B

SEWING

1. 45 Flip - 1a, 3a, 4a, 18c, 18d, 19a, 19b.
2. Piggyback Flip - 3b, 3c; 7a, 7b; 18a, 18b.
3. 45 Joint - 4 to 5, 6 to 7, 21 to 22.
4. Combination Half Rectangle Flip - Sew 11a to 11b. Sew 11 and 11ab together as a Half Rectangle.
5. Combination Flip - 2, 2a, 2b.
6. Sew 1 thru 24 together as shown to complete Unit B.

WILD GOOSE - UNIT C

SUBCUTTING

Fabric		Strip Width	Pc #	Size
Background	☐	9-1/2"	3	9-1/2" x 1-1/2"
			12	5-1/2" x 4-1/2"
			21	9-1/2" x 4-1/2"
		3-1/2"	1	3-1/2" x 2-1/2"
			2	3-1/2" x 2-1/2"
			5a	4-1/2" x 3-1/2"
			11	4-1/2" x 3-1/2"
			14	3-1/2" x 5-1/2"
			15	4-1/2" x 3-1/2"
			24	4-1/2" x 3-1/2"
		2-1/2"	10	4-1/2" x 1-1/2"
			20	6-1/2" x 2-1/2"
		1-1/2"	15b	1-1/2" x 1-1/2"
			16a,b,c	1-1/2" x 1-1/2"
			17a,b	1-1/2" x 1-1/2"
			18	8-1/2" x 1-1/2"
			23	2-1/2" x 1-1/2"
			25	1-1/2" x 9-1/2"
Goose body	☐	3-1/2"	1a	3-1/2" x 2-1/2"
			5	4-1/2" x 3-1/2"
			6	3-1/2" x 3-1/2"
			9b	3-1/2" x 3-1/2"
			11a	4-1/2" x 3-1/2"
		2-1/2"	7	2-1/2" x 1-1/2"
			19	6-1/2" x 2-1/2"
			21a	2-1/2" x 2-1/2"
			22	2-1/2" x 1-1/2"
		1-1/2"	2a	1-1/2" x 1-1/2"
			4	9-1/2" x 1-1/2"
			9a	1-1/2" x 1-1/2"
			13	9-1/2" x 1-1/2"
			14a	1-1/2" x 1-1/2"
			21b	1-1/2" x 1-1/2"
Goose wing	☐	4-1/2"	9	6-1/2" x 3-1/2"
		2-1/2"	6a	2-1/2" x 2-1/2"
			8	2-1/2" x 2-1/2"
			15a	2-1/2" x 2-1/2"
			16	2-1/2" x 3-1/2"
			17	2-1/2" x 3-1/2"
			19a	2-1/2" x 2-1/2"
Beak	☐	Scrap	22a	1-1/2" x 1-1/2"
			23a	2-1/2" x 1-1/2"

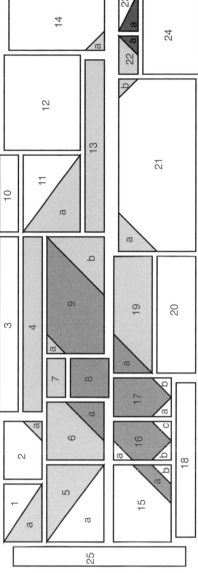

UNIT C

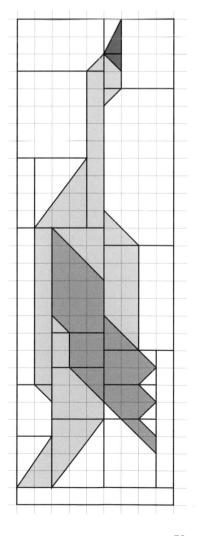

SEWING

1. 45 Flip - 2a, 6a, 9a, 9b, 14a, 16a, 16b, 16c, 17a, 17b, 19a, 21a, 21b, 22a.
2. Piggyback Flip - 15a, 15b.
3. Half Rectangle - 1, 1a; 5, 5a; 11, 11a; 23, 23a.
4. Sew 1 thru 25 together as shown to complete Unit C.

DOG - UNIT D

SUBCUTTING

Fabric		Strip Width	Pc #	Size
Background	☐	9-1/2"	26	3-1/2" x 9-1/2"
		3-1/2"	1	5-1/2" x 3-1/2"
			3	5-1/2" x 3-1/2"
			6	3-1/2" x 2-1/2"
			13	3-1/2" x 1-1/2"
			24	6-1/2" x 3-1/2"
		2-1/2"	11	2-1/2" x 2-1/2"
			25	18-1/2" x 2-1/2"
		1-1/2"	2a	1-1/2" x 1-1/2"
			4	4-1/2" x 1-1/2"
			5a,b	1-1/2" x 1-1/2"
			14b	1-1/2" x 1-1/2"
			15a,c	1-1/2" x 1-1/2"
			16	4-1/2" x 1-1/2"
			18	3-1/2" x 1-1/2"
			23	2-1/2" x 1-1/2"
Dog rear	◼	2-1/2"	1a	1-1/2" x 1-1/2"
			2	5-1/2" x 1-1/2"
			3a	1-1/2" x 1-1/2"
			5	4-1/2" x 2-1/2"
			8	3-1/2" x 2-1/2"
			9a	1-1/2" x 1-1/2"
			10	1-1/2" x 2-1/2"
			11a	1-1/2" x 1-1/2"
			12	3-1/2" x 1-1/2"
			14a	1-1/2" x 1-1/2"
Dog ear & middle	◼	2-1/2"	7	3-1/2" x 1-1/2"
			9	3-1/2" x 2-1/2"
			15	2-1/2" x 2-1/2"
			19	1-1/2" x 1-1/2"
			22a	1" x 1"
Dog head	◻	2-1/2"	13a	1-1/2" x 1-1/2"
			14	2-1/2" x 2-1/2"
			15b	1-1/2" x 1-1/2"
			17	2-1/2" x 1-1/2"
			20	1-1/2" x 1-1/2"
			21	3-1/2" x 2-1/2"
			22	2-1/2" x 1-1/2"
			23a	1-1/2" x 1-1/2"
			24a	1-1/2" x 1-1/2"

SEWING

1. 45 Flip - 1a, 2a, 3a, 5a, 5b, 9a, 11a, 13a, 14a, 14b, 15a, 15b, 15c, 22a, 23a, 24a.
2. 45 Joint - 17 to 18.
3. Sew 1 thru 26 together as shown to complete Unit D.

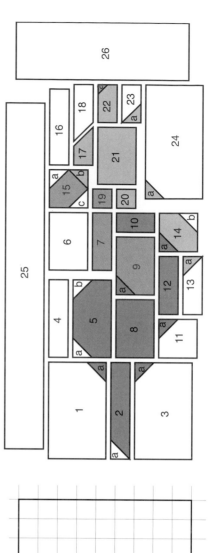

UNIT D

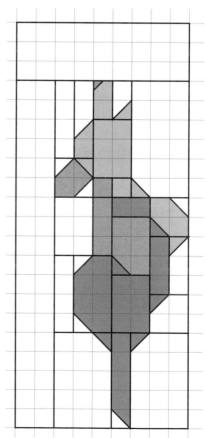

ASSEMBLY

SUBCUTTING

Fabric		Strip Width	# to Cut	Size
Background	☐	9-1/2"	2	9-1/2" x 13-1/2"
		3-1/2"	1	31-1/2" x 3-1/2"
			1	3-1/2" x 34-1/2"
			1	49-1/2" x 3-1/2"
		2-1/2"	24	2-1/2" x 2-1/2"
		1-1/2"	8	1-1/2" x 4-1/2"
Goose Tracks	■	2-1/2"	8	2-1/2" x 2-1/2"
			8	1-1/2" x 1-1/2"
		1-1/2"	26	1-1/2" x 1-1/2"

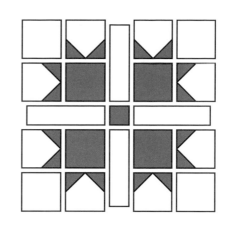

GOOSE TRACKS BLOCK (makes two)

1. 45 Flip - 1-1/2" Goose Track squares to two adjacent corners of eight 2-1/2" background squares.
2. Sew these together with the remaining 2-1/2" background squares, the 2-1/2" goose tracks squares, the remaining 1-1/2" goose tracks squares, and the 1-1/2" x 4-1/2" background pieces.

SEWING

1. Sew Unit A to Unit B. Stitch the 31-1/2" x 3-1/2" background across the top.
2. Sew a Goose Track block above one 9-1/2" x 13-1/2" background and below the other 9-1/2" x 13-1/2" background. Stitch these to the sides of AB as shown.
3. Sew Unit C to Unit D. Stitch CD below AB.
4. Sew the 49-1/2" x 3-1/2" background across the bottom.
5. Stitch the 3-1/2" x 34-1/2" background to the left side to complete the quilt.

FINISHING

Embroider feet on the geese.

We love our dogs! Notice little Davy Joe's head is cropped so we get a good picture of Brownie! Circa 1945

YAHOO
40" x 36"

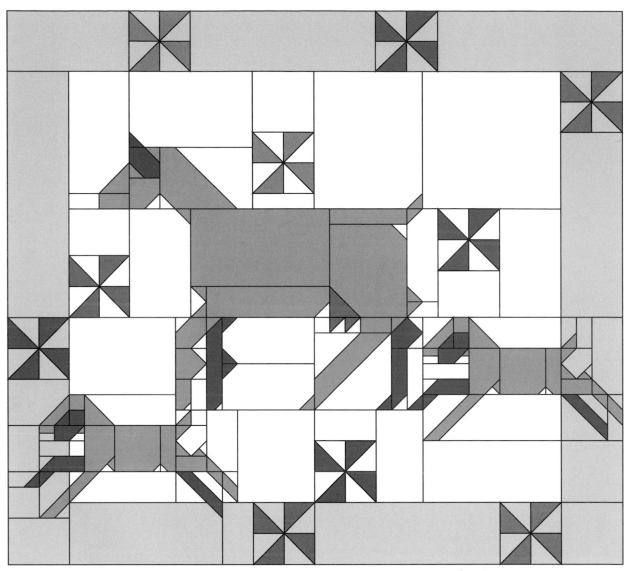

YARDAGE

1 yd.	☐	Background
1/4 yd.		Nanny body
1/8 yd.		Nanny ear & far legs
Scrap		Udder
1/4 yd.		Kid body
1/8 yd.		Kid ears & far legs
Scraps		Pinwheels
5/8 yd.		Border
1/2 yd.		Binding
1-1/3 yds.		Backing

CUTTING

Cut all strips crosswise as shown in Rotary Cutting. Cut the following strips, then refer to each Unit's cutting chart for sizes of pieces to cut from each strip. Pieces may be subcut from a wider strip.

Fabric		# of Strips	Strip Width
Background	☐	1	9-1/2"
		2	4-1/2"
		1	3-1/2"
		1	2-7/8"
		2	2-1/2"
		2	1-1/2"

Cutting, cont.

Fabric		# of Strips	Strip Width
Border	☐	3	4-1/2"
		1	2-7/8"
		1	2-1/2"
Nanny body		1	5-1/2"
		1	2-1/2"
Nanny ear & far legs		1	2-1/2"
Kid body		2	3-1/2"
Kid ear & far legs		1	3-1/2"
Pinwheel		Scraps	2-7/8"

PINWHEEL BLOCKS

Make four pinwheel blocks using pinwheel color and background.
Make six pinwheel blocks using pinwheel color and border fabric.

SUBCUTTING

Fabric		# to Cut	Size
Background	☐	8	2-7/8" x 2-7/8"
Border	☐	12	2-7/8" x 2-7/8"
Pinwheel scraps	■	20	2-7/8" x 2-7/8" (in multiples of 2)

SEWING

1. To make pinwheel half-squares, layer the squares with a pinwheel square on bottom and either a background or border on top.
2. Draw a diagonal line from corner to corner. Stitch 1/4" from diagonal line on both sides. Cut on the drawn line.
3. Open the squares up and press. Assemble as shown above to complete each pinwheel.

NANNY HEAD - UNIT A

SUBCUTTING

Fabric		Strip Width	Pc #	Size
Background	☐	9-1/2"	4	8-1/2" x 5-1/2"
			12	7-1/2" x 9-1/2"
			13	9-1/2" x 9-1/2"
		4-1/2"	1	4-1/2" x 8-1/2"
			8	5-1/2" x 4-1/2"
			9	4-1/2" x 4-1/2"
		2-1/2"	2	2-1/2" x 1-1/2"
			6a	1-1/2" x 1-1/2"
			7a	1-1/2" x 1-1/2"
			11	4-1/2" x 1-1/2"
			10	Pinwheel block

Cutting, cont.

Fabric		Strip Width	Pc #	Size
Nanny body		5-1/2"	7	5-1/2" x 4-1/2"
	☐	2-1/2"	1a	2-1/2" x 2-1/2"
			3	2-1/2" x 1-1/2"
			5a,b	1-1/2" x 1-1/2"
			6	2-1/2" x 2-1/2"
			12a	1-1/2" x 1-1/2"
Nanny ear & far legs	■	2-1/2"	4a	1-1/2" x 1-1/2"
			5	2-1/2" x 2-1/2"

UNIT A

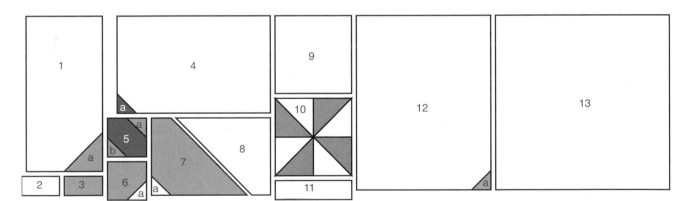

SEWING

1. 45 flip - 1a, 4a, 5a, 5b, 6a, 7a, 12a.
2. 45 Joint - 7 to 8.
3. Sew 1 thru 13 together as shown to complete Unit A.

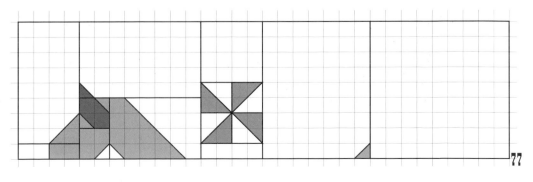

NANNY BODY - UNIT B

SUBCUTTING

Fabric		Strip Width	Pc #	Size
Background	☐	4-1/2"	1	4-1/2" x 3-1/2"
			3	4-1/2" x 7-1/2"
			12	4-1/2" x 3-1/2"
			13	4-1/2" x 7-1/2"
		2-1/2"	5	1-1/2" x 2-1/2"
			6a	1-1/2" x 1-1/2"
			8a	1-1/2" x 1-1/2"
			9	2-1/2" x 6-1/2"
			10	2-1/2" x 1-1/2"
			2	Pinwheel Block
			11	Pinwheel Block
Nanny body	▨	5-1/2"	4	9-1/2" x 5-1/2"
			6	8-1/2" x 2-1/2"
			7	5-1/2" x 1-1/2"
			8	5-1/2" x 6-1/2"
		1-1/2"	3a	1-1/2" x 1-1/2"
			5a,b	1-1/2" x 1-1/2"
			9a,b	1-1/2" x 1-1/2"
			10a	1-1/2" x 1-1/2"
Udder	▮	Scrap	8b	2-1/2" x 2-1/2"

c. 1915. Buster Jones, cousin of Ayliffe, and his pal. These "kids" would eat anything.

SEWING

1. 45 Flip - 3a, 5a, 5b, 6a, 8a, 8b, 9a, 9b, 10a.
2. Sew 1 thru 13 together as shown to complete Unit B.

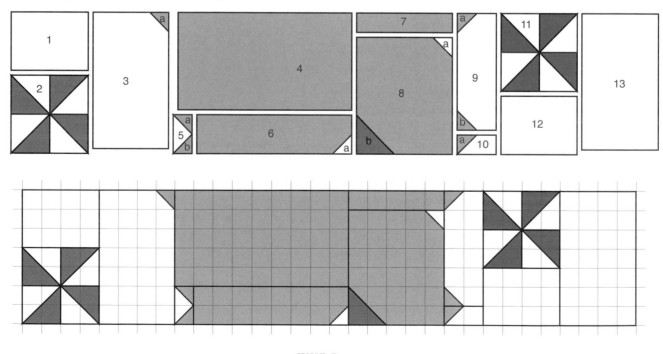

UNIT B

LEFT KID & BORDER - UNIT C

SUBCUTTING

Fabric		Strip Width	Pc #	Size
Background	☐	9-1/2"	3	7-1/2" x 5-1/2"
			37	5-1/2" x 6-1/2"
		3-1/2"	28	6-1/2" x 3-1/2"
			29	6-1/2" x 3-1/2"
		2-1/2"	6	6-1/2" x 2-1/2"
			21	7-1/2" x 2-1/2"
			32	2-1/2" x 2-1/2"
			34	2-1/2" x 4-1/2"
			35a,b	2-1/2" x 2-1/2"
		1-1/2"	10b	1-1/2" x 1"
			12	1-1/2" x 1-1/2"
			14b	1-1/2" x 1-1/2"
			15a	1" x 1"
			16a	1" x 1"
			21b	1-1/2" x 1-1/2"
			23a,b	1-1/2" x 1-1/2"
			24a,b	1-1/2" x 1-1/2"
			25a	1" x 1"
			26	1-1/2" x 2-1/2"
			27b	1" x 1"
			30	1-1/2" x 1-1/2"
			31	1-1/2" x 1-1/2"
			32d	1-1/2" x 1-1/2"
			36a,b	1-1/2" x 1-1/2"
Kid body	▨	3-1/2"	2a	2-1/2" x 2-1/2"
			4	1-1/2" x 1-1/2"
			6a	2-1/2" x 2-1/2"
			8	1-1/2" x 1"
			10a	1-1/2" x 1"
			14	2-1/2" x 3-1/2"
			14a	1-1/2" x 1-1/2"
			15	3-1/2" x 3-1/2"
			16	1-1/2" x 3-1/2"
			19b	2-1/2" x 2-1/2"
			21a	2-1/2" x 2-1/2"
			30a	1-1/2" x 1-1/2"
			32a,b,c	1-1/2" x 1-1/2"
			33	2-1/2" x 1-1/2"
			34a	1-1/2" x 1-1/2"
			35c	1-1/2" x 1-1/2"
			36	1-1/2" x 2-1/2"
Kid ear & far leg	▨	3-1/2"	2b	1-1/2" x 1-1/2"
			5	1-1/2" x 1-1/2"
			10	2-1/2" x 1-1/2"
			13	3-1/2" x 1-1/2"
			17a	1-1/2" x 1-1/2"
			19a	1-1/2" x 1-1/2"
			35	3-1/2" x 2-1/2"
			38a	1-1/2" x 1-1/2"

Subcutting, cont.

Fabric		Strip Width	Pc #	Size
Border	☐	4-1/2"	2	4-1/2" x 3-1/2"
			20	4-1/2" x 3-1/2"
			22	7-1/2" x 4-1/2"
			38	3-1/2" x 4-1/2"
			39	2-1/2" x 4-1/2"
		2-1/2"	7	2-1/2" x 3-1/2"
			9	1-1/2" x 1"
			11	2-1/2" x 1-1/2"
			13a	1-1/2" x 1-1/2"
			17	2-1/2" x 1-1/2"
			18	2-1/2" x 2-1/2"
			19	2-1/2" x 3-1/2"
			19c	1-1/2" x 1-1/2"
			1	Pinwheel Block
			40	Pinwheel Block
Nanny body	▨	5-1/2"	23	2-1/2" x 2-1/2"
			24	2-1/2" x 2-1/2"
		1-1/2"	25	1-1/2" x 2-1/2"
			27a	1-1/2" x 1-1/2"
			29b	1-1/2" x 1-1/2"
Nanny ear & far legs	▨	2-1/2"	27	1-1/2" x 6-1/2"
			28a,b	1-1/2" x 1-1/2"
			29a	1-1/2" x 1-1/2"

SEWING

1. 45 Flip - 6a, 13a, 15a, 16a, 17a, 19a, 23a, 23b, 24a, 24b, 25a, 27a, 27b, 28a, 28b, 29a, 29b, 32a, 32b, 34a, 35a, 36a, 36b, 38a.

2. Piggyback Flip - 2a, 2b; 19b, 19c; 21a, 21b; 35b, 35c.

3. Half Strip Flip - 10ab.

4. Half Square - 30, 30a.

5. Half Square Flip - 14ab, 32cd.

6. Sew 1 thru 40 together as shown to complete Unit C.

NOTE: Diagrams for Unit C are are the following page.

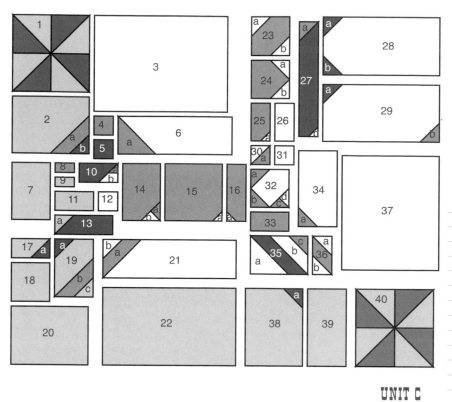

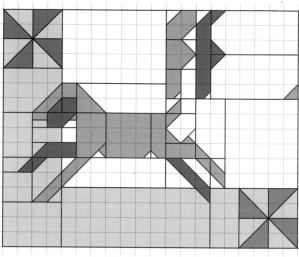

UNIT C

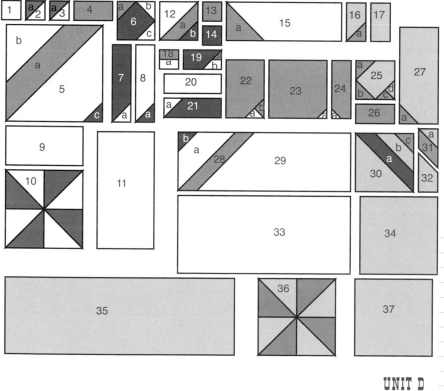

UNIT D

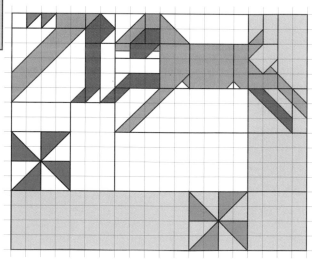

RIGHT KID & BORDER - UNIT D
SUBCUTTING

Fabric	Strip Width	Pc #	Size
Background □	9-1/2"	5	5-1/2" x 5-1/2"
	4-1/2"	33	9-1/2" x 4-1/2"
	3-1/2"	5b	3-1/2" x 3-1/2"
		11	3-1/2" x 6-1/2"
		29	8-1/2" x 3-1/2"
		28a	3-1/2" x 3-1/2"
	2-1/2"	9	4-1/2" x 2-1/2"
		12	2-1/2" x 2-1/2"
		15	6-1/2" x 2-1/2"
	1-1/2"	1	1-1/2" x 1-1/2"
		2	1-1/2" x 1-1/2"
		3	1-1/2" x 1-1/2"
		6b,c	1-1/2" x 1-1/2"
		7a	1-1/2" x 1-1/2"
		8	1-1/2" x 4-1/2"
		18a	1-1/2" x 1"
		19b	1-1/2" x 1"
		20	3-1/2" x 1-1/2"
		21a	1-1/2" x 1-1/2"
		22a	1-1/2" x 1-1/2"
		23a	1" x 1"
		24a	1" x 1"
		10	Pinwheel Block
Kid body ■	3-1/2"	12a	2-1/2" x 2-1/2"
		13	1-1/2" x 1-1/2"
		15a	2-1/2" x 2-1/2"
		16a	1-1/2" x 1-1/2"
		18	1-1/2" x 1"
		19a	1-1/2" x 1"
		22	2-1/2" x 3-1/2"
		22b	1-1/2" x 1-1/2"
		23	3-1/2" x 3-1/2"
		24	1-1/2" x 3-1/2"
		25a,b,c	1-1/2" x 1-1/2"
		26	2-1/2" x 1-1/2"
		27a	1-1/2" x 1-1/2"
		28	4-1/2" x 3-1/2"
		30c	1-1/2" x 1-1/2"
		31	1-1/2" x 2-1/2"
Kid ears & far legs ■	3-1/2"	8a	1-1/2" x 1-1/2"
		12b	1-1/2" x 1-1/2"
		14	1-1/2" x 1-1/2"
		19	2-1/2" x 1-1/2"
		21	3-1/2" x 1-1/2"
		28b	1-1/2" x 1-1/2"
		30a	3-1/2" x 3-1/2"
Nanny ear & far legs ■	2-1/2"	5c	1-1/2" x 1-1/2"
		6	2-1/2" x 2-1/2"
		7	1-1/2" x 4-1/2"
Udder ■	Scrap	2a	1-1/2" x 1-1/2"
		3a	1-1/2" x 1-1/2"

Subcutting, cont.

Fabric	Strip Width	Pc #	Size
Border ■	4-1/2"	30	3-1/2" x 3-1/2"
		34	4-1/2" x 4-1/2"
		35	12-1/2" x 4-1/2"
		37	4-1/2" x 4-1/2"
	2-1/2"	16	1-1/2" x 2-1/2"
		17	1-1/2" x 2-1/2"
		25	2-1/2" x 2-1/2"
		25d	1-1/2" x 1-1/2"
		27	2-1/2" x 5-1/2"
		30b	2-1/2" x 2-1/2"
		31a	1-1/2" x 1-1/2"
		32	1-1/2" x 2-1/2"
		36	Pinwheel Block
Nanny body ■	5-1/2"	5a	5-1/2" x 5-1/2"
	1-1/2"	4	2-1/2" x 1-1/2"
		6a	1-1/2" x 1-1/2"

SEWING

1. 45 Flip - 5c, 6a, 6b, 6c, 7a, 8a, 15a, 16a, 21a, 23a, 24a, 25a, 25b, 27a, 31a.
2. Piggyback Flip - 5a, 5b; 12a, 12b; 28a, 28b; 30a, 30b, 30c.
3. Half Square 2, 2a; 3, 3a.
4. Half Strip Flip - 19ab.
5. Half Square Flip - 22ab, 25cd.
6. 45 Joint - 28 to 29.
7. Sew 1 thru 37 together as shown to complete Unit D.

NOTE: Diagrams for Unit D are on the preceding page.

QUILT ASSEMBLY

SUBCUTTING

Fabric	Strip Width	# to Cut	Size
Border ■	4-1/2"	1	4-1/2" x 16-1/2"
		3	4-1/2" x 12-1/2"
		1	4-1/2" x 8-1/2"

SEWING

1. Sew Units A and B together.
2. Sew a border pinwheel and a 4-1/2" x 12-1/2" border piece together and sew to the right edge.
3. Sew a 4-1/2" x 16-1/2" border piece to the left edge.
4. Join together an 8-1/2" x 4-1/2" border piece, a border pinwheel, a 12-1/2" x 4-1/2" border piece, a border pinwheel, and a 12-1/2" x 4-1/2" border piece. Attach to the top of Units AB.
5. Sew Units C and D together. Attach below rest of quilt.

THREE LITTLE PIGS

53-1/2" x 41-1/2"

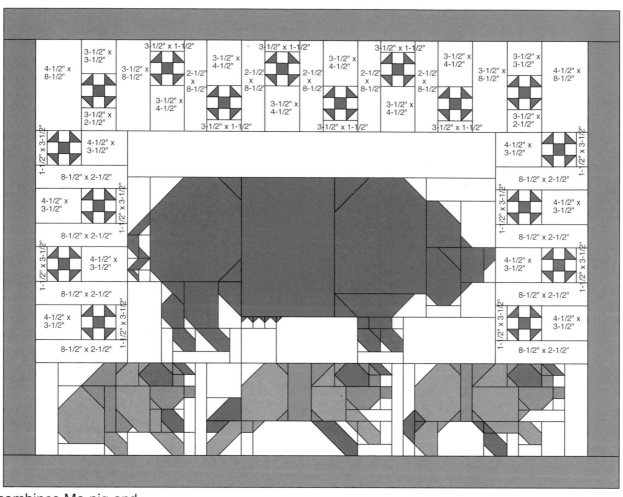

This quilt combines Ma pig and three little pigs with a Shoo-fly border. As each pig is made separately, it's easy to use them in a different quilt.

YARDAGE

1-3/4 yds.	☐	Background
1/3 yd.	■	Ma Pig head & rump
1/3 yd.	■	Ma Pig belly
1/3 yd.*	■	Piglet legs & rump
1/3 yd.*	■	Piglet face & belly
1/3 yd.*	■	Piglet ears & far legs
1/2 yd.	■	Border
1/2 yd.		Binding
2-2/3 yds.		Backing

Assorted scraps for sixteen 3-1/2" x 3-1/2" Shoo-fly Blocks

* Make piglets as shown or mix the fabrics as in the photo.

CUTTING

Cut all strips crosswise as shown in Rotary Cutting. Cut the following strips, then refer to each Unit's cutting chart for size of pieces to cut from each strip. Pieces may be subcut from a wider strip.

Fabric		# of Strips	Strip Width
Background	☐	2	4-1/2"
		1	3-1/2"
		2	2-1/2"
		3	1-1/2"
Ma Pig head & rump	■	1	8-1/2"
		1	1-1/2"
Ma Pig belly & far legs	■	1	8-1/2"

Cutting, cont.

Fabric		# of Strips	Strip Width
Piglet legs & rump	■	1	4-1/2"
		1	2-1/2"
		1	1-1/2"
Piglet face & belly	■	1	2-1/2"
		1	1-1/2"
Piglet ears & far legs	■	1	3-1/2"
Border	■	5	3-1/4"

MA PIG RUMP - UNIT A

SUBCUTTING

Fabric	Strip Width	Pc #	Size
Background ☐	4-1/2"	7a	3-1/2" x 3-1/2"
		8	3-1/2" x 7-1/2"
		16	1-1/2" x 3-1/2"
	2-1/2"	1	2-1/2" x 5-1/2"
		3	1-1/2" x 2-1/2"
		9a	2-1/2" x 2-1/2"
		12	2-1/2" x 3-1/2"
		14a	2-1/2" x 2-1/2"
		15	5-1/2" x 1-1/2"
	1-1/2"	1b	1-1/2" x 1-1/2"
		2a	1-1/2" x 1-1/2"
		4a,b	1-1/2" x 1-1/2"
		5a	1-1/2" x 1-1/2"
		5b	1" x 1"
		6	1-1/2" x 1-1/2"
		7d	1-1/2" x 1-1/2"
		9c	1-1/2" x 1-1/2"
		10a	1-1/2" x 1-1/2"
		13a,b	1-1/2" x 1-1/2"
		14b	1-1/2" x 1-1/2"
		17	1-1/2" x 3-1/2"
Ma Pig head & rump ▨	8-1/2"	7	8-1/2" x 9-1/2"

Cut Unit A piece 7 and Unit B piece 2 first, then subcut strip into 1-1/2", 2-1/2", and 3-1/2" strips

	3-1/2"	10	3-1/2" x 4-1/2"
		14	3-1/2" x 2-1/2"
	2-1/2"	1a	2-1/2" x 2-1/2"
		9b	2-1/2" x 2-1/2"
	1-1/2"	2	1-1/2" x 2-1/2"
		3a	1-1/2" x 1-1/2"
		4	2-1/2" x 1-1/2"
		5	1-1/2" x 1-1/2"
Ma Pig belly & far legs ▨	8-1/2"		Cut Unit B piece 1 first, then subcut into 3-1/2" & 2-1/2" strips
	3-1/2"	11	2-1/2" x 3-1/2"
	2-1/2"	7b,c	2-1/2" x 2-1/2"
		9	2-1/2" x 4-1/2"
		13	2-1/2" x 2-1/2"

UNIT A

SEWING

1. 45 Flip - 2a, 3a, 4a, 4b, 5a, 5b, 7a, 7b, 7c, 7d, 9c, 10a, 13a, 13b, 14a, 14b.
2. Flips in Order - 9a, 9b.
3. Piggyback Flip - 1a, 1b.
4. 45 Joint - 11 to 12.
5. Sew 1 thru 17 together as shown to complete Unit A.

MA PIG BELLY - UNIT B

SUBCUTTING

Fabric	Strip Width	Pc #	Size
Background ☐	2-1/2"	2b	2-1/2" x 2-1/2"
		4	3-1/2" x 2-1/2"
Ma Pig head ▨ & rump	8-1/2"	2*	8-1/2" x 10-1/2"
	2-1/2"	3	7-1/2" x 2-1/2"
Ma Pig belly ▨	8-1/2"	1*	8-1/2" x 12-1/2"
	3-1/2"	2a	3-1/2" x 3-1/2"
	2-1/2"	3a	2-1/2" x 2-1/2"

* Cut previously (page 83).

SEWING

1. 45 Flip - 2a, 2b, 3a.

2. 45 Joint - 3 to 4.

3. Sew 1 thru 4 together as shown to complete Unit B.

MA PIG HEAD - UNIT C

SUBCUTTING

Fabric	Strip Width	Pc #	Size
Background ☐	4-1/2"	3	3-1/2" x 4-1/2"
		9	3-1/2" x 3-1/2"
	2-1/2"	1	6-1/2" x 2-1/2"
		2a	2-1/2" x 2-1/2"
		7	1-1/2" x 2-1/2"
	1-1/2"	4b,c	1-1/2" x 1-1/2"
		8	3-1/2" x 1-1/2"
Ma Pig head ▨ & rump	3-1/2"	4	3-1/2" x 5-1/2"
		5	2-1/2" x 3-1/2"
	2-1/2"	6	1-1/2" x 2-1/2"
	1-1/2"	3a	1-1/2" x 1-1/2"
		9a	1-1/2" x 1-1/2"
Ma Pig belly ▨ & far legs	3-1/2"	2	3-1/2" x 4-1/2"
	2-1/2"	4a	2-1/2" x 2-1/2"

SEWING

1. 45 Flip - 2a, 3a, 4a, 4b, 4c, 9a.

2. 45 Joint - 6 to 7.

3. Sew 1 thru 9 together as shown to complete Unit C.

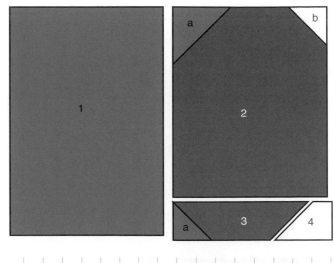

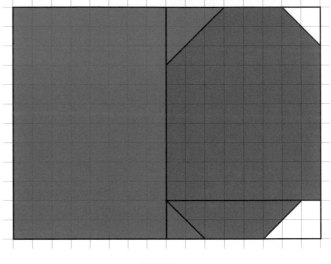

UNIT B

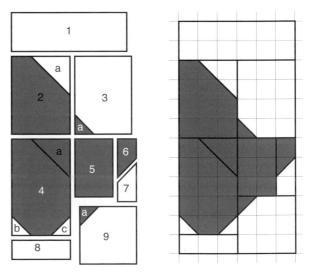

UNIT C

MA PIG FEET - UNIT D

SUBCUTTING

Fabric	Strip Width	Pc #	Size
Background	4-1/2"	1	3-1/2" x 3-1/2"
		5	7-1/2" x 4-1/2"
		12	8-1/2" x 4-1/2"
	1-1/2"	2,3,4	1-1/2" x 1-1/2"
		8	1-1/2" x 1-1/2"
		9b	1-1/2" x 1-1/2"
		10a,b	1-1/2" x 1-1/2"
		11	4-1/2" x 1-1/2"
Ma Pig head & rump	2-1/2"	7	2-1/2" x 1-1/2"
		10	2-1/2" x 2-1/2"
	1-1/2"	9a	1-1/2" x 1-1/2"
Ma Pig belly & far legs	2-1/2"	2a,b	1" x 1"
		3a,b	1" x 1"
		4a,b	1" x 1"
		5a	1" x 1"
		6	1-1/2" x 1-1/2"
		9	2-1/2" x 2-1/2"

SEWING

1. 45 Flip - 2a, 2b, 3a, 3b, 4a, 4b, 5a, 9a, 9b, 10a, 10b.

2. Sew 1 thru 12 together as shown to complete Unit D.

3. Sew A-D together.

4. Cut and sew a 32-1/2" x 4-1/2" background above Ma Pig.

SHOO-FLY BLOCK

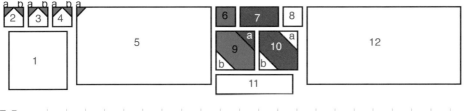

UNIT D

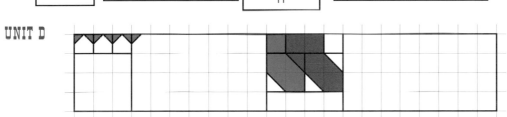

SHOO-FLY BORDER
CUTTING

Fabric	# of Strips	Strip Width
Background	1	8-1/2"
	1	4-1/2"
	3	3-1/2"
	2	1-7/8"
	3	1-1/2"

SEWING

Piece sixteen Shoo-fly blocks. Using the 1-7/8" squares of background and assorted fabrics, make Half Squares as shown on page 77. Sew these together with 1-1/2" background and color squares to make Shoo-fly blocks as shown above.

Assemble the two side borders and top border with the Shoo-fly blocks and the background pieces cut above, using the quilt diagram, page 82. Sew the side borders on, then the top.

SUBCUTTING

Fabric	Strip Width	# to cut	Size
Background	8-1/2"	15	8-1/2" x 2-1/2"
		2	8-1/2" x 1-1/2"
	4-1/2"	2	4-1/2" x 8-1/2"
	3-1/2"	14	3-1/2" x 4-1/2"
		14	3-1/2" x 1-1/2"
		2	3-1/2" x 3-1/2"
		2	3-1/2" x 2-1/2"
		2	3-1/2" x 8-1/2"
	1-7/8"	32	1-7/8" x 1-7/8"
	1-1/2"	64	1-1/2" x 1-1/2"
Assorted colors		16	1-1/2" x 1-1/2" (assorted, one for each two squares below)
		32	1-7/8" x 1-7/8" (assorted, multiples of 2)

PIGLET "NO NO"

SUBCUTTING

Fabric		Strip Width	Pc #	Size
Background	☐	3-1/2"	1	4-1/2" x 2-1/2"
			8a	2-1/2" x 2-1/2"
			16	1-1/2" x 3-1/2"
			18	4-1/2" x 2-1/2"
		2-1/2"	20	1-1/2" x 2-1/2"
		1-1/2"	5b	1-1/2" x 1-1/2"
			7	1-1/2" x 1-1/2"
			8c	1-1/2" x 1-1/2"
			9	4-1/2" x 1-1/2"
			11b	1-1/2" x 1-1/2"
			12b	1-1/2" x 1-1/2"
			14a	1-1/2" x 1-1/2"
			17a,b	1-1/2" x 1-1/2"
			19a	1-1/2" x 1-1/2"
Piglet legs & rump	▨	4-1/2"	8	4-1/2" x 5-1/2"
			11	3-1/2" x 4-1/2"
			19	3-1/2" x 2-1/2"
		2-1/2"	3	2-1/2" x 2-1/2"
			13	1-1/2" x 2-1/2"
			17	2-1/2" x 2-1/2"
		1-1/2"	4a,b	1-1/2" x 1-1/2"
			12a	1-1/2" x 1-1/2"
			14b	1-1/2" x 1-1/2"
Piglet face & belly	▨	2-1/2"	2	3-1/2" x 2-1/2"
			8b	2-1/2" x 2-1/2"
			11a	2-1/2" x 2-1/2"
			12	3-1/2" x 2-1/2"
		1-1/2"	3a	1-1/2" x 1-1/2"
			4c	1-1/2" x 1-1/2"
			5a	1-1/2" x 1-1/2"
			6	1-1/2" x 1-1/2"
			10	1-1/2" x 4-1/2"
			15	1-1/2" x 1-1/2"
Piglet ears & far legs	▨	3-1/2"	4	3-1/2" x 2-1/2"
			5	2-1/2" x 1-1/2"
			14	2-1/2" x 2-1/2"

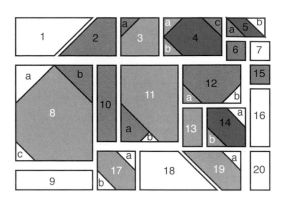

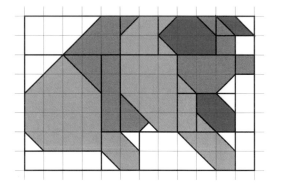

SEWING

1. 45 Flip - 3a, 4a, 4b, 4c, 5a, 5b, 8a, 8b, 8c, 12a, 12b, 14a, 14b, 17a, 17b, 19a.

2. 45 Flips in Order - Flip 11b to 11a. Flip this unit on 11.

3. 45 Joint - 1 to 2 and 18 to 19.

4. Sew 1 thru 20 together as shown to complete No, No Piglet.

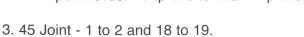

PIGLET "LET'S EAT"

SUBCUTTING

Fabric	Strip Width	Pc #	Size
Background ☐	3-1/2"	1	3-1/2" x 3-1/2"
		2a	2-1/2" x 2-1/2"
		16	3-1/2" x 1-1/2"
		19	8-1/2" x 3-1/2"
		23	3-1/2" x 1-1/2"
	2-1/2"	3a	1-1/2" x 2-1/2"
		3c	2-1/2" x 2-1/2"
		4a	2-1/2" x 2-1/2"
		18	1-1/2" x 2-1/2"
		20a	2-1/2" x 2-1/2"
		22	1-1/2" x 2-1/2"
	1-1/2"	8b	1-1/2" x 1-1/2"
		10	1-1/2" x 1-1/2"
		12b	1-1/2" x 1-1/2"
		14	1-1/2" x 1-1/2"
		21a,b	1-1/2" x 1-1/2"
Piglet legs & rump ▨	4-1/2"	3	3-1/2" x 3-1/2"
		4	4-1/2" x 5-1/2"
		11	3-1/2" x 3-1/2"
	2-1/2"	6	2-1/2" x 2-1/2"
		15	2-1/2" x 1-1/2"
		21	2-1/2" x 2-1/2"
	1-1/2"	7a,c	1-1/2" x 1-1/2"
		12a	1-1/2" x 1-1/2"
		17	1-1/2" x 1-1/2"
		19a	1-1/2" x 1-1/2"
		20b	1-1/2" x 1-1/2"
Piglet face & belly ▨	2-1/2"	5	2-1/2" x 5-1/2"
		6a	2-1/2" x 2-1/2"
		12	3-1/2" x 2-1/2"
	1-1/2"	4b,c	1-1/2" x 1-1/2"
		7b	1-1/2" x 1-1/2"
		8a	1-1/2" x 1-1/2"
		9	1-1/2" x 1-1/2"
		11a	1-1/2" x 1-1/2"
		13	1-1/2" x 1-1/2"
Piglet ears & far legs ▨	3-1/2"	2	3-1/2" x 2-1/2"
		3b	1-1/2" x 2-1/2"
		7	3-1/2" x 2-1/2"
		8	2-1/2" x 1-1/2"
		20	4-1/2" x 3-1/2"

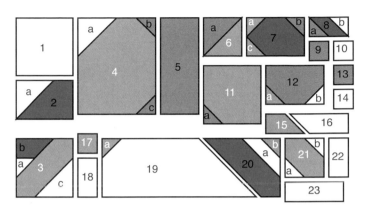

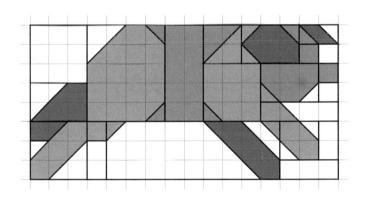

SEWING

1. 45 Flip - 2a, 3c, 4a, 4b, 4c, 7a, 7b, 7c, 8a, 8b, 11a, 12a, 12b, 19a, 21a, 21b.
2. Piggyback Flip - 20a, 20b.
3. 45 Joint - 15 to 16 and 19 to 20.
4. Half Square - 6, 6a.
5. Half Strip Flip - Sew 3a to 3b. Use this as a 45 Flip on 3.
6. Sew 1 thru 23 together as shown to complete Let's Eat Piglet.

PIGLET "MAYBE"

SUBCUTTING

Fabric	Strip Width	Pc #	Size
Background	3-1/2"	1a	2-1/2" x 2-1/2"
		14	4-1/2" x 3-1/2"
		20	2-1/2" x 3-1/2"
	2-1/2"	17	1-1/2" x 2-1/2"
		19	2-1/2" x 1-1/2"
		23	1-1/2" x 2-1/2"
	1-1/2"	5b	1-1/2" x 1-1/2"
		7	1-1/2" x 1-1/2"
		9b	1-1/2" x 1-1/2"
		11	1-1/2" x 1-1/2"
		12	4-1/2" x 1-1/2"
		13b	1-1/2" x 1-1/2"
		16a,b	1-1/2" x 1-1/2"
		18a,b	1-1/2" x 1-1/2"
		21	1-1/2" x 5-1/2"
Piglet legs & rump	4-1/2"	1	4-1/2" x 5-1/2"
		3	3-1/2" x 2-1/2"
		8	4-1/2" x 3-1/2"
		13	2-1/2" x 3-1/2"
	2-1/2"	18	2-1/2" x 2-1/2"
	1-1/2"	4a,b	1-1/2" x 1-1/2"
		9a	1-1/2" x 1-1/2"
		12a	1-1/2" x 1-1/2"
		14a	1-1/2" x 1-1/2"
		15	3-1/2" x 1-1/2"
Piglet face & belly	2-1/2"	3a	2-1/2" x 2-1/2"
		9	3-1/2" x 2-1/2"
	1-1/2"	1b,c	1-1/2" x 1-1/2"
		2	1-1/2" x 5-1/2"
		4c	1-1/2" x 1-1/2"
		5a	1-1/2" x 1-1/2"
		6	1-1/2" x 1-1/2"
		8a	1-1/2" x 1-1/2"
		10	1-1/2" x 1-1/2"
Piglet ears & far legs	3-1/2"	1d	1-1/2" x 1-1/2"
		4	3-1/2" x 2-1/2"
		5	2-1/2" x 1-1/2"
		13a	1-1/2" x 1-1/2"
		14b	1-1/2" x 1-1/2"
		15a	1-1/2" x 1-1/2"
		16	2-1/2" x 2-1/2"
		22	1-1/2" x 3-1/2"

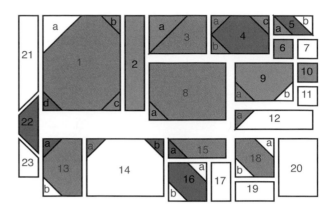

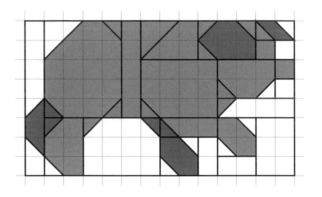

SEWING

1. 45 Flip - 1a, 1b, 1c, 1d, 3a, 4a, 4b, 4c, 5a, 5b, 8a, 9a, 9b, 12a, 13a, 13b, 14a, 14b, 15a, 16a, 16b, 18a, 18b.

2. 45 joint - 21 to 22 to 23.

3. Sew 1 thru 23 together as shown to complete Maybe Piglet.

FINAL ASSEMBLY

Sew the three little pigs together with a 1-1/2" x 8-1/2" background between each and a 2-1/2" x 8-1/2" background on each end. Sew this below Ma Pig.

BORDER
Sew on the 3-1/4" border.

DETAILS
Embroider tails on the three little pigs.

CHARLOTTE and WILBUR

24" x 24"

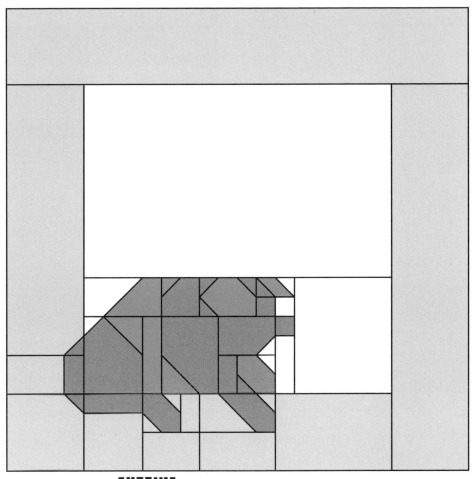

Designed by
Paula Cooper Black
Steamboat Springs, Colorado

Paula made a variation of No, No pig, page 86. The quilting makes this quilt come to life.

YARDAGE

1/3 yd.	☐	Background
1/8 yd.	■	Pig face & rump
1/8 yd.	■	Pig back & belly
3/8 yd.	☐	Border
1/3 yd.		Binding, piping
7/8 yd.		Backing

CUTTING

Cut all strips crosswise as shown in Rotary Cutting. Cut the following strips, then refer to each Unit's cutting chart for size of pieces to cut from each strip. Pieces may be subcut from a wider strip.

Fabric		# of Strips	Strip Width
Background	☐	1	10-1/2"
(cut a 16-1/2" x 10-1/2" piece first, then cut a 1-1/2" & 5-1/2" strip from remainder)			
Pig face & rump	■	1	3-1/2"
Pig back & belly	■	1	2-1/2"
Border	☐	2	4-1/2"
		1	2-1/2"

Milk, separate, feed the pigs, milk separate, feed the pigs... These were my chores.

WILBUR - UNIT A

SUBCUTTING

Fabric		Strip Width	Pc #	Size
Background	☐	5-1/2"	1	3-1/2" x 2-1/2"
			16	5-1/2" x 6-1/2"
		1-1/2"	5b	1-1/2" x 1-1/2"
			7	1-1/2" x 1-1/2"
			8a	1-1/2" x 1-1/2"
			11a	1-1/2" x 1-1/2"
			13a	1-1/2" x 1-1/2"
			15	1-1/2" x 3-1/2"
Pig face & rump	▨	3-1/2"	3	2-1/2" x 2-1/2"
			4a,b,c	1-1/2" x 1-1/2"
			5a	1-1/2" x 1-1/2"
			6	1-1/2" x 1-1/2"
			8	3-1/2" x 4-1/2"
			10	3-1/2" x 4-1/2"
			11	3-1/2" x 2-1/2"
			12	1-1/2" x 2-1/2"
			13b	1-1/2" x 1-1/2"
			14	1-1/2" x 1-1/2"
Pig back & belly	▦	2-1/2"	2	3-1/2" x 2-1/2"
			3a	1-1/2" x 1-1/2"
			4	3-1/2" x 2-1/2"
			5	2-1/2" x 1-1/2"
			8b	2-1/2" x 2-1/2"
			9	1-1/2" x 4-1/2"
			10a	2-1/2" x 2-1/2"
			13	2-1/2" x 2-1/2"

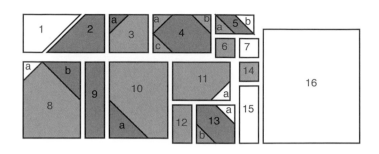

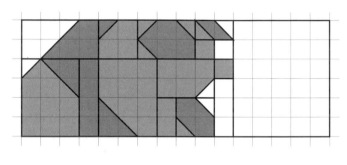

UNIT A

SEWING

1. 45 Flip - 3a, 4a, 4b, 4c, 5a, 5b, 8a, 8b, 10a, 11a, 13a, 13b.
2. 45 Joint - 1 to 2.
3. Sew 1 thru 16 together as shown to complete Unit A.

WILBUT - UNIT B

SUBCUTTING

Fabric		Strip Width	Pc #	Size
Border	☐	4-1/2"	2	3-1/2" x 2-1/2"
			1	4-1/2" x 14-1/2"
Pig face & rump	▨	3-1/2"	3	1-1/2" x 2-1/2"
			1a	1-1/2" x 1-1/2"

SEWING
1. 45 Flip - 1a.
2. Sew 1 thru 3 together as shown to complete Unit B.

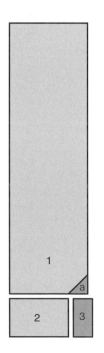
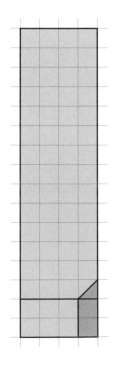

UNIT B

WILBUR - UNIT C

SUBCUTTING

Fabric	Strip Width	Pc #	Size
Border	4-1/2"	1	4-1/2" x 4-1/2"
		3	3-1/2" x 3-1/2"
		10	6-1/2" x 4-1/2"
	2-1/2"	4a,b	1-1/2" x 1-1/2"
		5	1-1/2" x 2-1/2"
		6	3-1/2" x 2-1/2"
		7	3-1/2" x 2-1/2"
		8a	1-1/2" x 1-1/2"
		9	4-1/2" x 2-1/2"
Pig face & rump	3-1/2"	1a	1-1/2" x 1-1/2"
		2	3-1/2" x 1-1/2"
		4	2-1/2" x 2-1/2"
		8	3-1/2" x 2-1/2"

SEWING

1. 45 Flip - 1a, 4a, 4b, 8a.
2. 45 Joint - 7 to 8.
3. Sew 1 thru 10 together as shown to complete Unit C.

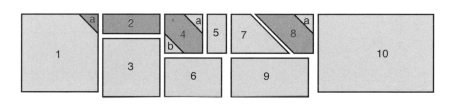

UNIT C

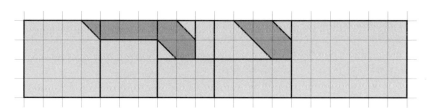

ASSEMBLY

SUBCUTTING

Fabric	Strip Width	Size
Background	10-1/2"	16-1/2" x 10-1/2" (See Cutting, page 89.)
Border	4-1/2"	4-1/2" x 20-1/2"
		4-1/2" x 24-1/2"

SEWING

1. Sew the 16-1/2" x 10-1/2" background above Unit A.
2. Optional piping - Fold two 1" strips of binding fabric in half lengthwise. With raw edges even, sew piping to top of Unit in Step 1. Fold under short edge of piping strip. Sew this strip to the left of the pig, beginning with the folded edge just above the pig's rear, and continuing to the top edge. Sew piping to the right edge of the Unit.
3. Sew Unit B to the left of Unit A.
4. Sew Unit C below AB.
5. Sew the 4-1/2" x 20-1/2" background to the right of ABC.
6. Sew the 4-1/2" x 24-1/2" background above ABC.

FINISHING

1. Embroider a spider in the upper right corner.
2. Quilt a spider web in the upper right corner.
3. Curl ribbon and stitch on for the pig's tail.

WHEN PIGS FLY...BY NIGHT!

24" x 20"

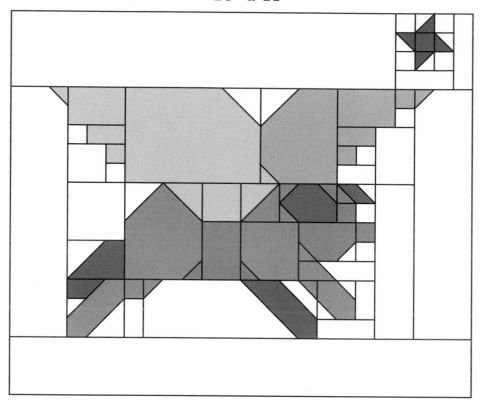

Designed by
Kathy Brunskill Faucett
Hayden, Colorado
This cute flying pig is a variation of the Let's Eat pig, page 87. Try modifying another of the animals to make it uniquely yours.

YARDAGE

1/2 yd.	☐	Background
1/4 yd.	▨	Pig legs & rump
1/8 yd.	▨	Pig face & belly
1/8 yd.	▪	Pig ears & far legs
1/4 yd.	▨	Left wing
1/4 yd.	▨	Right wing
Scrap	▪	Star
1/4 yd.		Binding
3/4 yd.		Backing

CUTTING

Fabric		# of Strips	Strip Width
Background	☐	1	4-1/2"
		2	3-1/2"
		1	1-1/2"
Pig legs & rump	▨	1	4-1/2"
Pig face & belly	▨	1	2-1/2"
Pig ears & far legs	▪	1	3-1/2"
Left wing	▨	1	5-1/2"
Right wing	▨	1	4-1/2"

I don't think this fellow could get off the ground. Not aerodynamic enough, but what a great guy to talk to.

PIGLET - UNIT A
SUBCUTTING

Fabric	Strip Width	Pc #	Size
Background ☐	4-1/2"	2a	2-1/2" x 2-1/2"
		4a	2-1/2" x 2-1/2"
		21a	2-1/2" x 2-1/2"
		25	2-1/2" x 8-1/2"
	3-1/2"	1	3-1/2" x 3-1/2"
		3c	2-1/2" x 2-1/2"
		17	3-1/2" x 1-1/2"
		20	8-1/2" x 3-1/2"
		24	3-1/2" x 1-1/2"
	1-1/2"	3b	2-1/2" x 1-1/2"
		9b	1-1/2" x 1-1/2"
		11	1-1/2" x 1-1/2"
		13b	1-1/2" x 1-1/2"
		15	1-1/2" x 1-1/2"
		19	1-1/2" x 2-1/2"
		22a,b	1-1/2" x 1-1/2"
		23	1-1/2" x 2-1/2"
Pig legs & rump ▨	4-1/2"	3	3-1/2" x 3-1/2"
		4	4-1/2" x 5-1/2"
		12	3-1/2" x 3-1/2"
		7	2-1/2" x 2-1/2"
		16	2-1/2" x 1-1/2"
		22	2-1/2" x 2-1/2"
		8a,c	1-1/2" x 1-1/2"
		13a	1-1/2" x 1-1/2"
		18	1-1/2" x 1-1/2"
		20a	1-1/2" x 1-1/2"
		21b	1-1/2" x 1-1/2"
Pig face & belly ▨	2-1/2"	6	2-1/2" x 3-1/2"
		13	3-1/2" x 2-1/2"
		4c	1-1/2" x 1-1/2"
		8b	1-1/2" x 1-1/2"
		9a	1-1/2" x 1-1/2"
		10	1-1/2" x 1-1/2"
		12a	1-1/2" x 1-1/2"
		14	1-1/2" x 1-1/2"
Pig ears & far legs ▨	3-1/2"	2	3-1/2" x 2-1/2"
		3a	2-1/2" x 1-1/2"
		8	3-1/2" x 2-1/2"
		9	2-1/2" x 1-1/2"
		21	4-1/2" x 3-1/2"
Left wing ☐	5-1/2"	4b	2-1/2" x 2-1/2"
		5	2-1/2" x 2-1/2"
		7a	2-1/2" x 2-1/2"

SEWING

1. 45 Flip - 2a, 3c, 4a, 4b, 4c, 7a, 8a, 8b, 8c, 9a, 9b, 12a, 13a, 13b, 20a, 22a, 22b.

2. Piggyback Flip - 21a, 21b.

3. 45 Joint - 16 to 17 and 20 to 21.

4. Half Strip Flip - Sew 3a to 3b. Use this as a 45 Flip on 3.

5. Sew 1 thru 24 together as shown to complete Let's Eat flying piglet, Unit A.

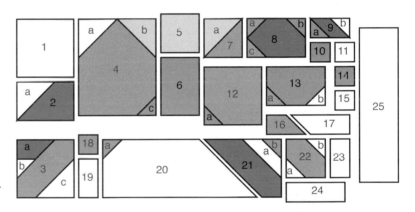

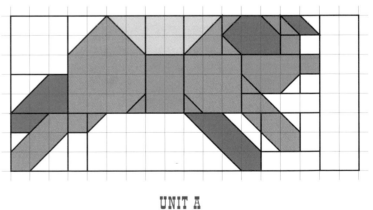

UNIT A

PIGLET WINGS - UNIT B

SUBCUTTING

Fabric		Strip Width	Pc #	Size
Background	☐	3-1/2"	4	2-1/2" x 2-1/2"
			7a	2-1/2" x 2-1/2"
			8a	2-1/2" x 2-1/2"
			16	2-1/2" x 3-1/2"
		1-1/2"	2	1-1/2" x 1-1/2"
			6	1-1/2" x 1-1/2"
			11	1-1/2" x 1-1/2"
			14	1-1/2" x 1-1/2"
			15	2-1/2" x 1-1/2"
Left wing	☐	5-1/2"	1	3-1/2" x 2-1/2"
			3	2-1/2" x 1-1/2"
			5	1-1/2" x 1-1/2"
			7	7-1/2" x 5-1/2"
			8b	1-1/2" x 1-1/2"
Right wing	☐	4-1/2"	8	4-1/2" x 5-1/2"
			9	3-1/2" x 2-1/2"
			10	1-1/2" x 1-1/2"
			12	2-1/2" x 1-1/2"
			13	1-1/2" x 1-1/2"

SEWING

1. 45 Flip - 7a, 8a, 8b.

2. Sew 1 thru 16 together as shown to complete Unit B.

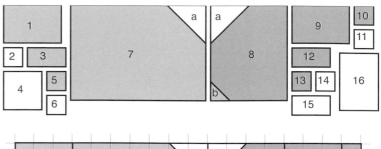

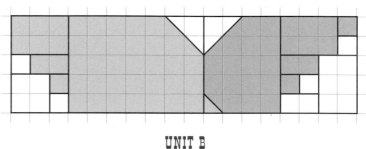

UNIT B

STAR BORDER - UNIT C

SUBCUTTING

Fabric Color		Strip Width	Pc #	Size
Background	☐	4-1/2"	4	1-1/2" x 4-1/2"
			1	20-1/2" x 4-1/2"
		3-1/2"	3	3-1/2" x 1-1/2"
		1-1/2"	Cut 8	1-1/2" x 1-1/2"
Star	■		Cut 5	1-1/2" x1-1/2"

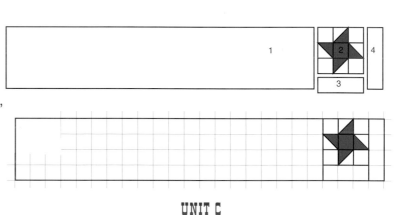

UNIT C

SEWING

1. 45 Flip - Make four Half Squares using 1-1/2" star squares and 1-1/2" background squares. Use the remaining 1-1/2" squares with these to make the star unit (piece 2).
2. Sew 1 thru 4 together as shown to complete Unit C.

ASSEMBLY

SUBCUTTING

Fabric		Strip Width	# to Cut	Size
Background	☐	3-1/2"	2	3-1/2" x 13-1/2"
			1	24-1/2" x 3-1/2"
Left wing	☐	5-1/2"	1	1-1/2" x 1-1/2"
Right wing	☐	4-1/2"	1	1-1/2" x 1-1/2"

SEWING

1. Sew Unit A below Unit B.
2. 45 Flip a 1-1/2" Left wing square to upper right corner of a 3-1/2" x 13-1/2" background, and sew this to the left of Unit AB.
3. 45 Flip a 1-1/2" Right wing square to upper left corner of a 3-1/2" x 13-1/2" Background, and sew this to the right of AB.
4. Sew 24-1/2" x 3-1/2" Background below AB.
5. Sew Unit C above AB to complete the quilt top.

FINISHING

Embroider a tail on the pig.

I DARE YOU
43" x 22"

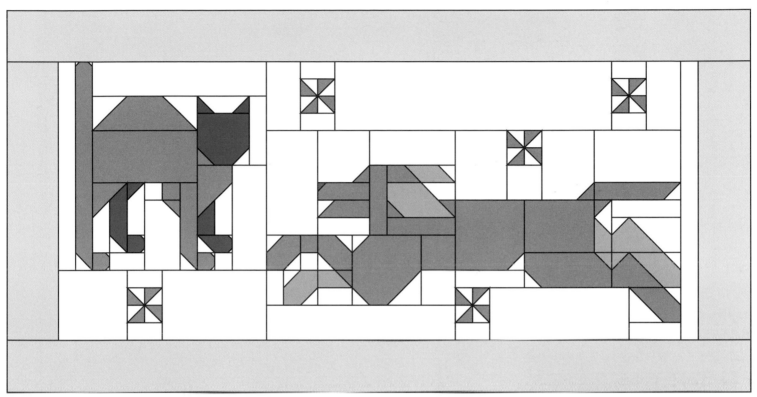

This quilt combines the cat Hiss 'n' Fuss, the dog Peppy, and pinwheel blocks. Directions are given for each animal separately with instructions to put the quilt together. Note the substitutions in the dog for the pinwheels. The other cat, Misty, page 102, could be used instead of Hiss 'n' Fuss.

YARDAGE

3/4 yd.	☐	Background
1/8 yd.	▨	Cat body
1/8 yd.	▨	Cat head & far legs
1/4 yd.	▨	Dog body
1/8 yd.	▨	Dog ears & far legs
Scrap	▨	Dog Nose
Scraps		Pinwheels
1/2 yd.	☐	Border
1/3 yd.		Binding
1-3/8 yds.		Backing

CUTTING

Cut all strips crosswise as shown in Rotary Cutting. Cut the following strips, then refer to each Unit's cutting chart for size of pieces to cut from each strip. Pieces may be subcut from a wider strip.

Fabric		#of Strips	Strip Width
Background	☐	2	4-1/2"
		2	2-1/2"
		1	1-7/8"
		3	1-1/2"
Cat body	▨	1	3-1/2"
Cat head & far legs	▨	1	3-1/2"
Dog body	▨	1	4-1/2"
		1	1-1/2"
Dog ears & far legs	▨	1	2-1/2"
Nose	▨	1	scrap

Aunties little darlings! She never noticed the mischief they got into.

HISS 'N' FUSS CAT – UNIT A

SUBCUTTING

Fabric		Strip Width	Pc #	Size
Background	☐	2-1/2"	3a,b	2-1/2" x 2-1/2"
			5b	1-1/2" x 4-1/2"
			9	2-1/2" x 1-1/2"
			12	2-1/2" x 4-1/2"
			22	2-1/2" x 6-1/2"
			23	10-1/2" x 2-1/2"
		1-1/2"	1	1-1/2" x 12-1/2"
			2a	1-1/2" x 1-1/2"
			5a	1-1/2" x 1-1/2"
			6	1-1/2" x 3-1/2"
			10	1-1/2" x 1-1/2"
			13a	1-1/2" x 1-1/2"
			14	3-1/2" x 1-1/2"
			15b	1-1/2" x 1-1/2"
			16	1-1/2" x 4-1/2"
			18	1-1/2" x 3-1/2"
			19a	1-1/2" x 1-1/2"
			21	1-1/2" x 1-1/2"
			2b,c	1" x 1"
			7a,b	1" x 1"
			8a,b	1" x 1"
			19b,c	1" x 1"
			20a,b	1" x 1"
Cat body	▨	3-1/2"	2	1-1/2" x 12-1/2"
			3	6-1/2" x 2-1/2"
			4	6-1/2" x 3-1/2"
			5c	2-1/2" x 2-1/2"
			8	1-1/2" x 1-1/2"
			11	1-1/2" x 1-1/2"
			12a	1-1/2" x 1-1/2"
			15a	1-1/2" x 1-1/2"
			13	1-1/2" x 5-1/2"
			17	2-1/2" x 3-1/2"
			20	1-1/2" x 1-1/2"
Cat head & far legs	▩	3-1/2"	5	1-1/2" x 4-1/2"
			6a	1-1/2" x 1-1/2"
			7	1-1/2" x 1-1/2"
			14a,b	1-1/2" x 1-1/2"
			15	3-1/2" x 3-1/2"
			18a	1-1/2" x 3-1/2"
			19	2-1/2" x 1-1/2"

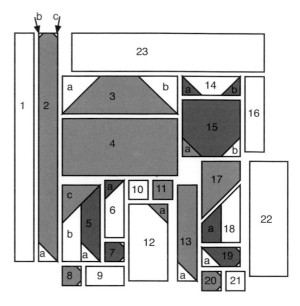

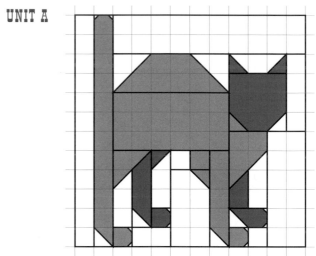

UNIT A

SEWING

1. To give Hiss & Fuss' feet and tail a "rounded" look, use the ten 1" background squares as flips for pieces 2, 7, 8, 19 & 20.

2. 45 Flip - 2a, 3a, 3b, 6a, 12a, 13a, 14a, 14b, 15a, 15b, 19a.

3. Half Strip - 45 Flip 5a to 5. Sew 5 and 5b together. 45 Flip 5c to it.

4. Half Strip - Sew the 18 and 18a pieces together.

5. 45 Joint - 17 to 18.

6. Sew 1 thru 23 together as shown to complete Unit A, Hiss 'n' Fuss.

UNIT B

SUBCUTTING

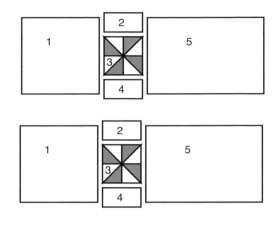

Fabric	Strip Width	Pc#	Size
Background ☐	4-1/2"	1	4-1/2" x 4-1/2"
		5	6-1/2" x 4-1/2"
	1-1/2"	2	2-1/2" x 1-1/2"
		4	2-1/2" x 1-1/2"
	1-7/8"	3	(cut 10)1-7/8" x 1-7/8"
Assorted scraps (cut 2 of each) ▫ ◼		3	(cut 10)1-7/8" x 1-7/8"

UNIT B

SEWING

1. Make five pinwheel blocks to be used in Units B, C, and D. Using the 1-7/8" background and color squares, layer the squares with a color on bottom and a background on top, right sides together. Draw a diagonal line from corner to corner. Stitch 1/4" from diagonal line on both sides. Cut on the diagonal line. Press open. Repeat with remaining squares. Assemble the pinwheels.

2. Sew 1 thru 5 together as shown, using a pinwheel block for 3.

UNIT C

SUBCUTTING

Fabric	Strip Width	Pc#	Size
Background ☐	4-1/2"	1	2-1/2" x 4-1/2"
		5	16-1/2" x 4-1/2"
		9	2-1/2" x 4-1/2"
	1-1/2"	2	2-1/2" x 1-1/2"
		4	2-1/2" x 1-1/2"
		6	2-1/2" x 1-1/2"
		8	2-1/2" x 1-1/2"
		3	pinwheel
		7	pinwheel

SEWING

Sew 1 thru 9 together as shown, using pinwheels for 3 and 7.

UNIT C

PEPPY - UNIT D

SUBCUTTING

Fabric		Strip Width	Pc #	Size
Background	☐	4-1/2"	1	3-1/2" x 6-1/2"
			2	3-1/2" x 3-1/2"
			5	3-1/2" x 1-1/2"
			24*	8-1/2" x 4-1/2" (see note)
			25	5-1/2" x 3-1/2"
			28	4-1/2" x 1-1/2"
			33	4-1/2" x 1-1/2"
			38*	10-1/2" x 3-1/2" (see note)
		2-1/2"	6	5-1/2" x 2-1/2"
			9b	2-1/2" x 1-1/2"
			16	1-1/2" x 2-1/2"
			19	2-1/2" x 1-1/2"
			20c	2-1/2" x 2-1/2"
			22	2-1/2" x 2-1/2"
			23	11-1/2" x 2-1/2"
			30	1-1/2" x 2-1/2"
			35	3-1/2" x 2-1/2"
			39b	2-1/2" x 2-1/2"
		1-1/2"	4a	1-1/2" x 1-1/2"
			8a	1-1/2" x 1-1/2"
			12a,b	1-1/2" x 1-1/2"
			14	1-1/2" x 1-1/2"
			15a,b	1-1/2" x 1-1/2"
			17a,b	1-1/2" x 1-1/2"
			20a,b	1-1/2" x 1-1/2"
			26a	1-1/2" x 1-1/2"
			27a	1-1/2" x 1-1/2"
			32a	1-1/2" x 1-1/2"
			34a	1-1/2" x 1-1/2"
			37a	1-1/2" x 1-1/2"
			39a	1-1/2" x 1-1/2"
			40	3-1/2" x 1-1/2"

Fabric		Strip Width	Pc #	Size
Dog body	■	4-1/2"	3	3-1/2" x 1-1/2"
			4	3-1/2" x 1-1/2"
			7	2-1/2" x 1-1/2"
			10	4-1/2" x 1-1/2"
			11	1-1/2" x 4-1/2"
			12	2-1/2" x 2-1/2"
			15	2-1/2" x 2-1/2"
			20	4-1/2" x 4-1/2"
			21	2-1/2" x 2-1/2"
			27	4-1/2" x 4-1/2"
			29	4-1/2" x 3-1/2"
			32	5-1/2" x 2-1/2"
			36	3-1/2" x 2-1/2"
			39	3-1/2" x 2-1/2"
		1-1/2"	2a	1-1/2" x 1-1/2"
			9a	1-1/2" x 1-1/2"
			9c	2-1/2" x 1-1/2"
			13	1-1/2" x 1-1/2"
			18a	1-1/2" x 1-1/2"
			24a	1-1/2" x 1-1/2"
			26	5-1/2" x 1-1/2"
			30a	1-1/2" x 1-1/2"
Dog ears & far legs	■	2-1/2"	8	3-1/2" x 1-1/2"
			9	4-1/2" x 2-1/2"
			17	2-1/2" x 2-1/2"
			18	2-1/2" x 1-1/2"
			31	1-1/2" x 2-1/2"
			32b	1-1/2" x 1-1/2"
			34	3-1/2" x 2-1/2"
			36a	1-1/2" x 1-1/2"
			37	3-1/2" x 2-1/2"
Nose	■	Scrap	3a	1" x 1"

*Note - If using pinwheels in the dog block, cut these pieces instead. For Piece 24 cut two 3-1/2" x 4-1/2" and one 2-1/2" x 2-1/2". For Piece 38 cut one 2-1/2" x 1-1/2" and one 8-1/2" x 3-1/2".

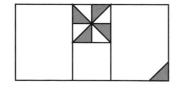

alternate piece 24

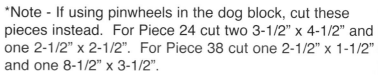

alternate piece 38

SEWING

1. 45 Flip - 2a, 3a, 4a, 8a, 9a, 12a, 12b, 15a, 15b, 17a, 17b, 18a, 20a, 20b, 20c, 24a, 26a, 27a, 30a, 32a, 32b, 34a, 36a, 37a, 39a, 39b.

2. 45 Joint - 7 to 8, 30 to 31, 34 to 35, 36 to 37.

3. Half Strip Flip - Sew the 9b and 9c pieces together. 45 Flip this to 9.

4. If using a pinwheel in 24 and 38, assemble as shown below left and substitute for 24 and 38.

5. Sew 1 thru 40 together as shown to complete Unit D, Peppy.

QUILT ASSEMBLY

1. Sew Unit A to Unit B and Unit C to Unit D. Sew A-B to C-D. Add a 1-1/2" x 16-1/2" background to the right side.

2. Sew a 3-1/2" border around the quilt.

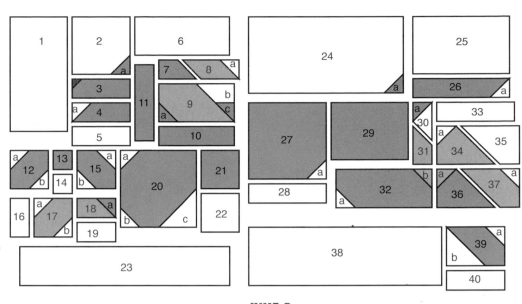

UNIT D

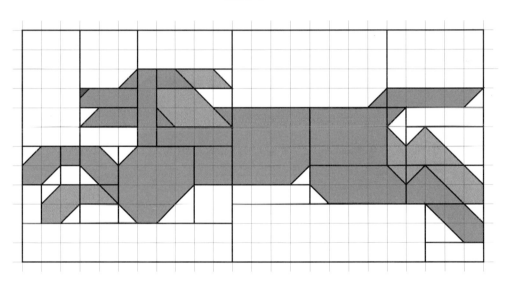

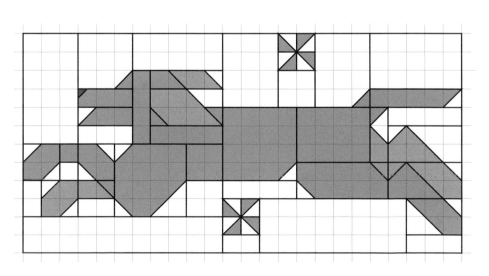

Peppy with the alternate pieces 24 and 38

INDIVIDUAL PET YARDAGE

HISS 'N' FUSS
12" X 12"

1/4 yd. Background
1/8 yd. Cat body
1/8 yd. Cat head & far legs

PEPPY
12" X 24"

1/3 yd. Background
1/4 yd. Dog body
2-1/2" strip Dog ears & far legs
Scrap Nose

WHEN YOU WISH UPON A STAR

31-1/2" x 27-1/2"

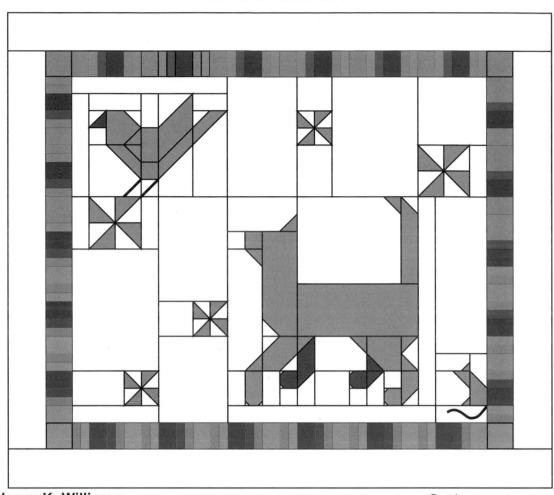

Designed by **Nancy K. Williams**
Steamboat Springs, Colorado

Combine a cat, mouse, bird, and some pinwheels and the result is this fun quilt.

YARDAGE

7/8 yd.	⬜	Background
*1/8 yd.	🟩	Cat body
1/8 yd.	🟦	Cat far legs
*1/8 yd.	🟩	Bird body
*1/8 yd.	🟩	Bird wing
1-1/2" strip	🟩	Mouse
Scrap	🟥	Bird beak
Scraps	🟩	Pinwheels
*1/3 yd.		Binding
1 yd.		Backing

* For a scrap binding, purchase 1/4 yd. and no binding.

100

CUTTING

Cut all strips crosswise as shown in Rotary Cutting. Cut the following strips, then refer to each Unit's cutting chart for dimensions of pieces to cut from each strip. Pieces may be sub-cut from a wider strip.

Fabric		# of Strips	Strip Width
Background	⬜	1	5-1/2"
		1	4-1/2"
		4	2-3/4"
		1	2-1/2"
		3	1-1/2"
Cat body	🟩	1	3-1/2"
Cat far legs	🟦	1	1-1/2"

Cutting, cont.

Fabric		# of Strips	Strip Width
Bird body	🟩	1	2-1/2"
Bird wing	🟩	1	2-1/2"

This cat ruled the doghouse. She seemed to say, "Come on, you little pups, just try me!"

BIRD - UNIT A

SUBCUTTING

Fabric		Strip Width	Pc #	Size
Background	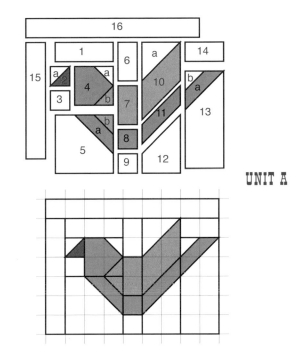	5-1/2"	10a	2-1/2" x 2-1/2"
			13	2-1/2" x 5-1/2"
		4-1/2"	5	3-1/2" x 3-1/2"
			12	2-1/2" x 3-1/2"
		1-1/2"	1	3-1/2" x 1-1/2"
			2a	1-1/2" x 1-1/2"
			3	1-1/2" x 1-1/2"
			4a	1-1/2" x 1-1/2"
			6	1-1/2" x 2-1/2"
			9	1-1/2" x 1-1/2"
			13b	1-1/2" x 1-1/2"
			14	2-1/2" x 1-1/2"
			15	1-1/2" x 6-1/2"
			16	9-1/2" x 1-1/2"
Bird body		2-1/2"	4	2-1/2" x 2-1/2"
			5a	2-1/2" x 2-1/2"
			8	1-1/2" x 1-1/2"
			11	2-1/2" x 3-1/2"
			13a	2-1/2" x 2-1/2"
Bird wing		2-1/2"	4b	1-1/2" x 1-1/2"
			5b	1-1/2" x 1-1/2"
			7	1-1/2" x 2-1/2"
			10	2-1/2" x 4-1/2"
Beak Scrap			2	1-1/2" x 1-1/2"

SEWING

1. 45 Flip - 4a, 4b, 10a.
2. Half Square - 2, 2a.
3. Piggyback Flip - 5a, 5b; 13a, 13b.
4. 45 Joint - 10 to 11 to 12.
5. Sew 1 thru 16 together as shown to complete the bird, Unit A.

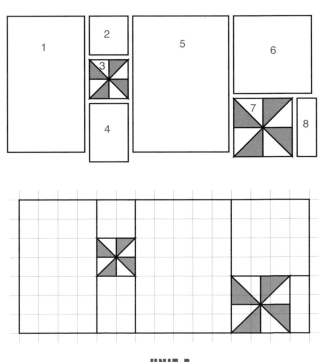

UNIT A

UNIT B

SUBCUTTING

Fabric		Strip Width	Pc #	Size
Background		5-1/2"	2	2-1/2" x 2-1/2"
			5	5-1/2" x 7-1/2"
		4-1/2"	1	4-1/2" x 7-1/2"
			4	2-1/2" x 3-1/2"
			6	4-1/2" x 4-1/2"
		2-1/2"	3 (cut 6)	1-7/8" x 1-7/8"
			7 (cut 4)	2-3/8" x 2-3/8"
		1-1/2"	8	1-1/2" x 3-1/2"
Pinwheel (assorted)		Scraps	(cut 6)	1-7/8" x 1-7/8"
			(cut 4)	2-3/8" x 2-3/8"

SEWING

1. Make three 2" pinwheels with the 1-7/8" squares and two 3" pinwheels with the 2-3/8" squares to be used in Units B and C. See instructions on page 77.
2. Using a small Pinwheel for 3 and a large Pinwheel for 7, sew 1 thru 8 together as shown to complete Unit B.

UNIT B

MISTY CAT - UNIT D

For Unit C, see page 103

SUBCUTTING

Fabric		Strip Width	Pc #	Size
Background	☐	5-1/2"	12	6-1/2" x 5-1/2"
			18	2-1/2" x 2-1/2"
		4-1/2"	1	4-1/2" x 2-1/2"
		2-1/2"	4	2-1/2" x 7-1/2"
			17	3-1/2" x 2-1/2"
		1-1/2"	2	1-1/2" x 1-1/2"
			5a	1-1/2" x 1-1/2"
			6a,b	1-1/2" x 1-1/2"
			7	1-1/2" x 2-1/2"
			8a,b	1" x 1"
			9	1-1/2" x 2-1/2"
			10a,b	1" x 1"
			11	1-1/2" x 1-1/2"
			13a	1-1/2" x 1-1/2"
			16	1-1/2" x 2-1/2"
			19a,b	1" x 1"
			20	1-1/2" x 1-1/2"
			22	1-1/2" x 2-1/2"
			23	1-1/2" x 2-1/2"
			24	1-1/2" x 1-1/2"
			25a,b	1" x 1"
			26a	1-1/2" x 1-1/2"
			27	1-1/2" x 12-1/2"
			28	12-1/2" x 1-1/2"
Cat body	▨	3-1/2"	1a	1-1/2" x 1-1/2"
			3	1-1/2" x 1-1/2"
			4a,b	1-1/2" x 1-1/2"
			5	2-1/2" x 6-1/2"
			6	2-1/2" x 2-1/2"
			8	1-1/2" x 2-1/2"
			12a	1-1/2" x 1-1/2"
			13	1-1/2" x 5-1/2"
			14	7-1/2" x 3-1/2"
			15a	1-1/2" x 1-1/2"
			17a	1-1/2" x 1-1/2"
			21	2-1/2" x 2-1/2"
			22a,b	1-1/2" x 1-1/2"
			25	1-1/2" x 1-1/2"
			26	1-1/2" x 2-1/2"
Cat far legs	▤	1-1/2"	10	1-1/2" x 1-1/2"
			15	1-1/2" x 3-1/2"
			19	1-1/2" x 1-1/2"
			21a	1-1/2" x 1-1/2"
			23a	1-1/2" x 1-1/2"

SEWING

1. To give the cat's feet a "rounded" look, use the eight 1" x 1" background squares and apply them as half inch flips for feet pieces 8, 10, 19, and 25.

2. 45 Flip - 1a, 4a, 4b, 5a, 6a, 6b, 12a, 13a, 15a, 17a, 21a, 22a, 22b, 23a, 26a.

3. 45 Joint - 15 to 16.

4. Sew 1 thru 28 together as shown to complete Unit D.

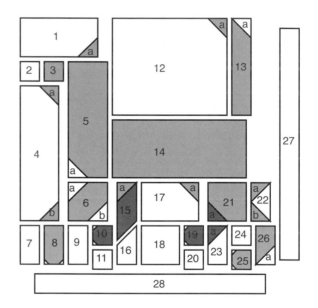

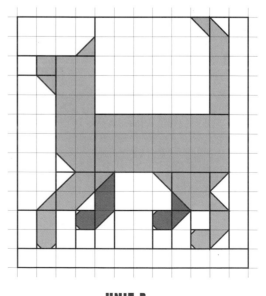

UNIT D

UNIT C

SUBCUTTING

Fabric	Strip Width	Pc #	Size
Background ☐	5-1/2"	4	5-1/2" x 7-1/2"
		7	5-1/2" x 1-1/2"
		9	2-1/2" x 2-1/2"
		11	4-1/2" x 5-1/2"
	4-1/2"	8	4-1/2" x 6-1/2"
	2-1/2"	5	3-1/2" x 2-1/2"
	1-1/2"	1	1-1/2" x 3-1/2"
		3	1-1/2" x 3-1/2"
		2	large pinwheel
		6	small pinwheel
		10	small pinwheel

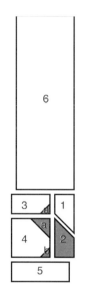

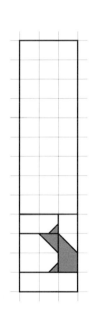

UNIT C

SEWING

1. Using a large Pinwheel for 2 and small Pinwheels for 6 and 10, sew 1 thru 11 together as shown to complete Unit C.

MOUSE - UNIT E

SUBCUTTING

Fabric	Strip Width	Pc #	Size
Background ☐	4-1/2"	6	3-1/2" x 9-1/2"
	2-1/2"	4	2-1/2" x 2-1/2"
	1-1/2"	1	1-1/2" x 2-1/2"
		3	2-1/2" x 1-1/2"
		5	3-1/2" x 1-1/2"
Mouse ▨	1-1/2"	2	1-1/2" x 2-1/2"
		3a,4b	1" x 1"
		4a	1-1/2" x 1-1/2"

SEWING

1. 45 Flip - 3a, 4a, 4b.
2. 45 Joint - 1 to 2.
3. Sew 1 thru 6 together as shown to complete Unit E.

UNIT E

ASSEMBLY
Sew Unit A to Unit B. Sew Units C, D, and E together. Sew A-B to C-D-E.

BORDERS
PIECED BORDER 1
Cut several assorted strips from colored fabrics 3/4" to 1-1/4" wide. Sew the strips together, lengthwise, into a strip set. Cut 2" segments from the strip set. Stitch the segment together to make border strips. Make two 20-1/2" units for the sides and two 24-1/2" units for the top and bottom, adding a 2" square to each corner.
BORDER 2
Sew on a border of 2-3/4" background strips.

DETAILS
Embroider legs on the bird, a tail on the mouse, and a collar on the cat. The bird and cat have button eyes. This cat has a bell on her collar.

THE MICE
15" x 8"

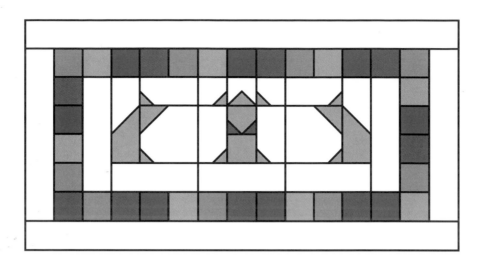

Make these three mice into a small wall hanging, or use them with other animals or in borders as seen on pages 26 and 100. Each mouse is 3" x 4" finished and can be made using scraps.

YARDAGE

1/4 yd.	☐	Background
Scraps	▨	Body (3 fabrics used)
Scraps		Border (assorted)
3/8 yd.		Backing and Binding

CUTTING

Cut all strips crosswise as shown in Rotary Cutting. Cut the following strips, then refer to each Unit's cutting chart for size of pieces to cut from each strip. Pieces may be subcut from a wider strip.

Fabric	# of Strips	Strip Width
Background ☐	1	2-1/2"
	2	1-1/2"

This is Art, our dear neighbor, Chuck Fulton's bull. Chuck still feeds every day with his team of horses, Fred and Sonny.

LEFT & RIGHT MICE - UNITS A & C
These are mirror image mice. Cut one of each piece for each mouse.

SUBCUTTING

Fabric		Strip Width	Pc #	Size
Background	☐	2-1/2"	1	1-1/2" x 2-1/2"
			3	2-1/2" x 1-1/2"
			4	2-1/2" x 2-1/2"
			5	3-1/2" x 1-1/2"
Body	▦	Scraps	2	1-1/2" x 2-1/2"
			3a,4b	1" x 1"
			4a	1-1/2" x 1-1/2"

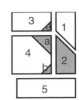

SEWING
1. 45 Flip - 3a, 4a, 4b.
2. 45 Joint - 1 to 2.
3. Sew 1 to 5 together as shown to complete each mouse,
   Unit A and Unit C.

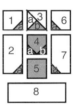

CENTER MOUSE - UNIT B

SUBCUTTING

Fabric		Strip Width	Pc #	Size
Background	☐	2-1/2"	1	1-1/2" x 1-1/2"
			2	1-1/2" x 2-1/2"
			3,3a	1-1/2" x 1-1/2"
			6	1-1/2" x 1-1/2"
			7	1-1/2" x 2-1/2"
			8	3-1/2" x 1-1/2"
Body	▦	Scraps	1a,2a	1" x 1"
			6a,7a	1" x 1"
			3b	1-1/2" x 1-1/2"
			4	1-1/2" x 1-1/2"
			5	1-1/2" x 1-1/2"
Hands		Scraps	4a,b	1" x 1"

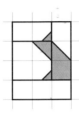

SEWING
1. 45 Flip - 1a, 2a, 4a, 4b, 6a, 7a.
2. Triple Flip - Make a Half Square from 3a and 3b; 45 Flip it to 3.
3. Sew 1 thru 8 together to complete Mouse B.

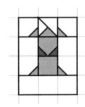

ASSEMBLY
1. Sew Unit B between Units A and C.
2. Add a 1-1/2" x 4-1/2" background to each end.

BORDER
1. Cut 34 assorted 1-1/2" squares from scraps.
2. Stitch two units of four squares. Sew these to the sides of the quilt.
3. Stitch two units of thirteen squares. Sew to the top and bottom.
4. Add a 1-1/2" background border on all four sides.

DETAILS
Embroider whiskers and tails on the mice.

BARNYARD MUSICIANS
63" x 70"

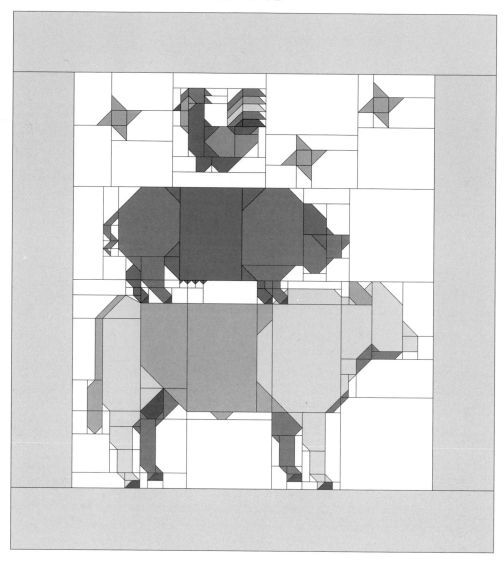

YARDAGE

2-1/4 yds.	☐	Background
5/8 yd.	☐	Bull head, rump & shoulder
3/8 yd.	☐	Bull body, tail
1/4 yd.	☐	Bull far legs
1/8 yd.	☐	Bull hooves
1/3 yd.	☐	Pig head & rump
1/3 yd.	☐	Pig belly & far legs
1/8 yd.	☐	Rooster body
1/4 yd.	☐	Rooster wing
Scraps		Feathers (assorted)
1/8 yd.	☐	Stars
1-7/8 yds.	☐	Border
5/8 yd.		Binding
3-7/8 yds.		Backing

CUTTING

Cut all strips crosswise as shown in Rotary Cutting. Cut the following strips, then refer to each Unit's cutting chart for size of pieces to cut from each strip. Pieces may be subcut from a wider strip.

Fabric	# of Strips	Strip Width
Background ☐	2	12-1/2"
	1	6-1/2"
	2	4-1/2"
	3	3-1/2"
	4	2-1/2"
	3	1-1/2"
Bull head, rump & shoulder ☐	1	9-1/2"
	1	4-1/2"
	1	2-1/2"

Cutting, cont.

Fabric	# of Strips	Strip Width
Bull body, tail ☐	1	9-1/2"
	1	2-1/2"
Bull far legs ☐	1	4-1/2"
Bull hooves ☐	1	3-1/2"
Pig head & rump ☐	1	8-1/2"
Pig belly & far legs ☐	1	8-1/2"
Rooster body ☐	1	2-1/2"
Rooster wing ☐	1	4-1/2"
Star ☐	1	2-1/2"
Border ☐	7	8-1/2"

BULL SECTION

Make the bull as explained on pages 21-24, substituting and adding the pieces below. This is necessary because the bottom of the pig and the top of the bull merge and there are no chickens with this bull.

BULL RUMP - UNIT A

SUBCUTTING

Fabric		Strip Width	Pc #	Size
Background ☐			1	omit
		12-1/2"	*13	5-1/2" x 5-1/2"
		3-1/2"	*2	6-1/2" x 3-1/2"
			*5	3-1/2" x 8-1/2"
			*10	2-1/2" x 3-1/2"
		2-1/2"	*7	2-1/2" x 4-1/2"
			*20	7-1/2" x 2-1/2"
			23	7-1/2" x 2-1/2"
		1-1/2"	24a	1-1/2" x 1-1/2"
			25	1-1/2" x 1-1/2"
Pig belly	■	2-1/2"	4b	1-1/2" x 1-1/2"
& far legs			24	2-1/2" x 1-1/2"
			26	1-1/2" x 1-1/2"

*Substitute for same number pieces on page 21.

SEWING

1. Make Unit A, 2 thru 22, as explained on page 21. Be sure to substitute the 2-13 pieces cut above for those numbers on page 21.
2. 45 Flip - 4b, 24a.
3. Sew 23 thru 26 together as shown. Stitch this above 2-22 to complete Unit A.

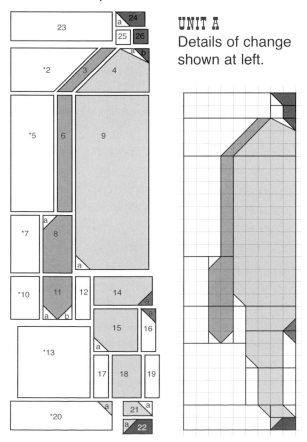

UNIT A
Details of change shown at left.

BULL REAR LEGS - UNIT B

SUBCUTTING

Fabric		Strip Width	Pc #	Size
Background ☐			1	omit
		2-1/2"	15a	2-1/2" x 2-1/2"
			16	2-1/2" x 2-1/2"
		1-1/2"	11a	1-1/2" x 1-1/2"
			12	2-1/2" x 1-1/2"
			13	1-1/2" x 1-1/2"
			14a	1-1/2" x 1-1/2"
			15b	1-1/2" x 1-1/2"
Pig head	■	3-1/2"	11	3-1/2" x 1-1/2"
& rump			15	3-1/2" x 2-1/2"
Pig belly &	■	8-1/2"	13a,b	1" x 1"
far legs		2-1/2"	14	1-1/2" x 2-1/2"
Bull hooves	■	3-1/2"	14b	1-1/2" x 1-1/2"
			15c	1-1/2" x 1-1/2"

SEWING

1. Make Unit B, 2 thru 10, as explained on page 22.
2. 45 Flip - 11a, 13a, 13b, 14a, 14b, 15a, 15b, 15c.
3. Sew 11 thru 16 together as shown. Stitch this above 2-10 to complete Unit B.

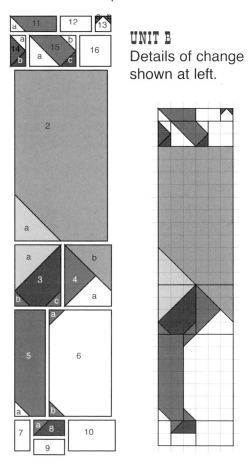

UNIT B
Details of change shown at left.

BULL MIDDLE - UNIT C

SUBCUTTING

Fabric		Strip Width	Pc #	Size
Background	☐		1	omit
		12-1/2"	9*	12-1/2" x 9-1/2"
		3-1/2"	13	7-1/2" x 3-1/2"
			16c	1-1/2" x 1-1/2"
		2-1/2"	12	2-1/2" x 2-1/2"
		1-1/2"	10	1-1/2" x 1-1/2"
			11	1-1/2" x 1-1/2"
Pig head	■	2-1/2"	15	1-1/2" x 1-1/2"
& rump			16a	1-1/2" x 1-1/2"
Pig belly	■	8-1/2"	10a,b	1" x 1"
& far legs			11a,b	1" x 1"
			13a	1" x 1"
		2-1/2"	14	1-1/2" x 1-1/2"
			16	2-1/2" x 2-1/2"
Bull hooves	■	3-1/2"	16b	1-1/2" x 1-1/2"

* Substitute for same numbered piece on page 22.

SEWING

1. Make Unit C, 2 thru 9, as explained on page 22.
   Be sure to substitute the #9 piece.
2. 45 Flip - 10a, 10b, 11a, 11b, 13a, 16a, 16b, 16c.
3. Sew 10 thru 16 together as shown.
   Stitch this to 2-9 to complete Unit C.

BULL FRONT LEGS - UNIT D

SUBCUTTING

Fabric		Strip Width	Pc #	Size
Background	☐		1	omit
			2a	omit
			2e	omit
		1-1/2"	20	1-1/2" x 1-1/2"
			21a,c	1-1/2" x 1-1/2"
	☐		22	7-1/2" x 1-1/2"
			23a	1-1/2" x 1-1/2"
Bull head		9-1/2"	*2	9-1/2" x 14-1/2"
& shoulder	■		21b,d	1-1/2" x 1-1/2"
			23	7-1/2" x 2-1/2"
Pig head	■	2-1/2"	19	1-1/2" x 1-1/2"
& rump			21	2-1/2" x 2-1/2"
Bull hooves		3-1/2"	21e	1-1/2" x 1-1/2"

*Substitute for same number piece on page 23.

SEWING

1. Make Unit D, 2 thru 18, as explained on page 23.
   Be sure to substitute the number 2 piece.
2. 45 Flip - 21e, 23a.
3. Half Square Flip - 21a, 21b; 21c, 21d.
4. Sew 19 thru 23 together as shown. Stitch this
   above 2-18 to complete Unit D.

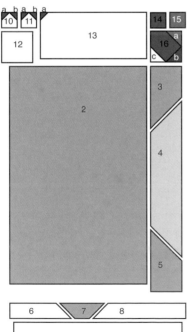

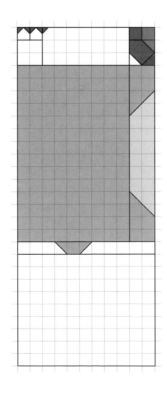

UNIT C
Details of change
shown at left.

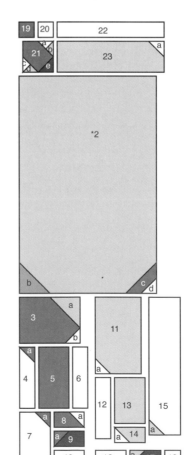

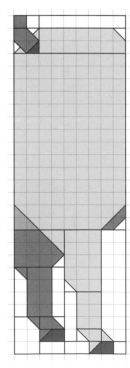

UNIT D
Details of change
shown at left.

BULL HEAD - UNIT E

Make Unit E as explained on page 24, substituting a 12-1/2" x 12-1/2" background for piece 15.

BULL ASSEMBLY

Sew Units A thru E together.

PIG SECTION

Make the Ma Pig as explained on pages 83-85, substituting and adding the pieces below. This is necessary because the bottom of the pig and the top of the bull merge.

PIG RUMP - UNIT A

SUBCUTTING

Fabric	Strip Width	Pc #	Size
Background ☐	4-1/2"	*8	3-1/2" x 3-1/2"
	2-1/2"	*12	2-1/2" x 2-1/2"
		9c	omit
		10a	omit
		13a,b	omit
		14a,b	omit
		15	omit
		16	omit
		17	omit

Pig head & rump ▦ Cut Unit A, piece 7 and Unit B piece 2 first, then subcut strip into 1-1/2", 2-1/2", and 3-1/2" strips.

	3-1/2"	*10	3-1/2" x 3-1/2"
		14	omit

Pig belly & far legs ▦ Cut Unit B piece 1 first, then cut others.

	8-1/2"	*9	2-1/2" x 3-1/2"
		13	omit

*Substitute for same number pieces on page 83.

SEWING

1. Sew 1 thru 12 together as explained on page 83 to complete Unit A. Be sure to substitute the pieces above.

PIG - UNITS B & C

Make Units B and C as explained on page 84.

PIG - UNIT D

Unit D as shown on page 85 was constructed as part of the bull. Do not make another Unit D.

PIG ASSEMBLY

Subcutting

Fabric	Strip Width	# to Cut	Size
Background	12-1/2"	1	4-1/2" x 12-1/2"
☐		1	11-1/2" x 12-1/2"

1. Sew Units A thru C together.
2. Sew a 4-1/2" x 12-1/2" background to the left of the pig.
3. Sew an 11-1/2" x 12-1/2" background to the right of the pig.
4. Stitch the pig above the bull.

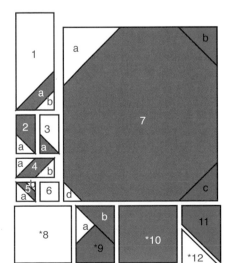

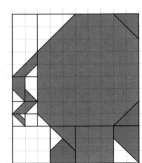

PIG UNIT A
Details of change shown at left.

ROOSTER & STAR SECTION

LEFT STAR - UNIT A

SUBCUTTING

Fabric	Strip Width	Pc #	Size
Background ☐	6-1/2"	1	5-1/2" x 7-1/2"
		2	5-1/2" x 8-1/2"
		3	8-1/2" x 5-1/2"
		7	8-1/2" x 6-1/2"
	4-1/2"	6	6-1/2" x 4-1/2"
	2-1/2"	5	2-1/2" x 2-1/2"
Star ■	2-1/2"	1a	2-1/2" x 2-1/2"
		3a	2-1/2" x 2-1/2"
		4	2-1/2" x 2-1/2"
		5a	2-1/2" x 2-1/2"
		6a	2-1/2" x 2-1/2"

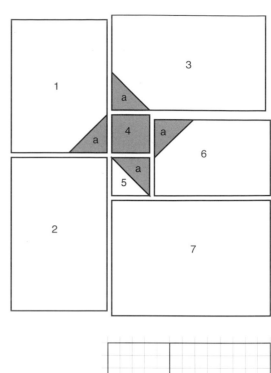

SEWING

1. 45 Flip - 1a, 3a, 5a, 6a.
2. Sew 1 thru 7 together as shown to complete Unit A.

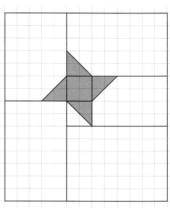

ROOSTER - UNIT B

SUBCUTTING

Fabric	Strip Width	Pc #	Size
Background ☐	2-1/2"	28	12-1/2" x 2-1/2"
		29	12-1/2" x 2-1/2"

SEWING

1. Make a rooster as explained on pages 12-13. For piece 28 use a 12-1/2" x 2-1/2" background.
2. Sew piece 29 on top to complete Unit B.

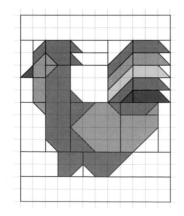

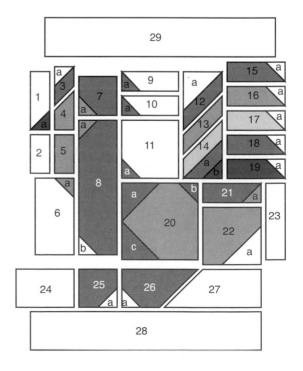

CENTER STAR - UNIT C

SUBCUTTING

Fabric		Strip Width	Pc #	Size
Background	☐	12-1/2"	1	12-1/2" x 8-1/2"
		6-1/2"	7	6-1/2" x 5-1/2"
		4-1/2"	2	4-1/2" x 4-1/2"
			3	4-1/2" x 3-1/2"
		2-1/2"	4	8-1/2" x 2-1/2"
			6	2-1/2" x 3-1/2"
Star	▨	2-1/2"	2a	2-1/2" x 2-1/2"
			4a	2-1/2" x 2-1/2"
			5	2-1/2" x 2-1/2"
			6a	2-1/2" x 2-1/2"
			7a	2-1/2" x 2-1/2"

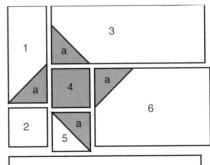

SEWING

1. 45 Flip - 2a, 4a, 6a, 7a.
2. Sew 1 thru 7 together as shown to complete Unit C.

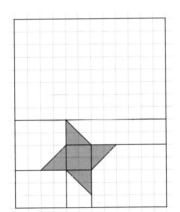

RIGHT STAR - UNIT D

SUBCUTTING

Fabric		Strip Width	Pc #	Size
Background	☐	12-1/2"	7	10-1/2" x 8-1/2"
		4-1/2"	3	8-1/2" x 3-1/2"
			6	6-1/2" x 4-1/2"
		2-1/2"	1	2-1/2" x 5-1/2"
			2	2-1/2" x 2-1/2"
			5	2-1/2" x 2-1/2"
Star	▨	2-1/2"	1a	2-1/2" x 2-1/2"
			3a	2-1/2" x 2-1/2"
			4	2-1/2" x 2-1/2"
			5a	2-1/2" x 2-1/2"
			6a	2-1/2" x 2-1/2"

SEWING

1. 45 Flip - 1a, 3a, 5a, 6a.
2. Sew 1 thru 7 together as shown to complete Unit D.
3. Sew Units A thru D together to complete the rooster section.
4. Sew the rooster above the pig.

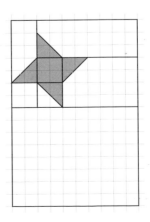

BORDER

Sew 8-1/2" strips to the sides of the quilt, then the top and bottom, piecing as necessary.

Also from ANIMAS QUILTS PUBLISHING

WEAVER FEVER by Jackie Robinson $ 6.50
Bargello type quilts in a woven design. Easy.

TESSELLATIONS by Jackie Robinson $ 12.00
Geometric shapes forming a repeating pattern.
Inspired by M.C. Escher.

DINING DAZZLE by Jackie Robinson $ 16.00
A collection of 20 placemats and 4 table runners.

SIMPLY LANDSCAPES by Judy Sisneros $ 14.00
Turn your favorite scene into a quilt with ease.

STARBOUND by Susan Dillinger $ 8.00
Coordinated treeskirts, stockings, table runners, etc.

CHILDREN'S ZOO by Barbara Morgan $ 18.00
A safari of animals in quilts and accessories.

TERRIFIC TRIANGLES by Shelly Burge $ 18.00
Slick tricks for scrappy half-square triangles.

QUILTS in the tradition of FRANK LLOYD WRIGHT $ 19.00
by Jackie Robinson
Eighteen designs based on Wright's art glass windows.

SENSATIONAL STARS by Gail Garber $ 15.00
Create spectacular star quilts.

EASY TRADITIONAL QUILTING by Lora Rocke $ 15.00
Continuous quilting designs with transfer instructions.

BARGELLO BY THE BLOCK by Joan Waldman $ 14.00
New variations on the Weaver Fever strip set.

SQUARE IN A SQUARE by Jodi Barrows $ 16.00
Cutting and piecing technique with super results.

THE VEST YEAR EVER by Jackie Boroff $ 16.00
12 vests - one for each month.

HOLIDAY HEROES by Jaynette Huff and Carole Stearle $ 16.00
Paper pieced characters for the seasons.

PERENNIAL PATCHWORK by Jackie Robinson $ 11.00
A garden of flower blocks in eight different "sets".

BINDING MITER TOOL $ 4.00
Make mitered corners on quilt bindings
easy and perfect every time.

PLEASE ADD POSTAGE:

$ 3.00 FOR 1 - 2 BOOKS
$ 4.00 FOR 3 - 4 BOOKS
$ 5.00 FOR 5 - 6 BOOKS

BINDING TOOL ONLY
POSTAGE - $1.00

THANK YOU!

**Animas
Quilts
Publishing**
**600 Main Ave.
Durango, CO. 81301
(970) 247-2582**